Emails
from an
Asshole

Real People
Being Stupid

Emails
from an
Asshole

Real People
Being Stupid

John Lindsay

STERLING

New York / London
www.sterlingpublishing.com

STERLING and the distinctive Sterling logo are registered trademarks of Sterling Publishing Co., Inc.

Lindsay, John.
   Emails from an asshole : real people being stupid / John Lindsay.
      p. cm.
   ISBN 978-1-4027-7827-8
   1. Personals—Humor. 2. Electronic mail messages—Humor. I. Title.
   PN6231.P36L56 2010
   818'.602—dc22
                2010003578

2 4 6 8 10 9 7 5 3 1

Published by Sterling Publishing Co., Inc.
387 Park Avenue South, New York, NY 10016
© 2010 by John Lindsay
Distributed in Canada by Sterling Publishing
c/o Canadian Manda Group, 165 Dufferin Street
Toronto, Ontario, Canada M6K 3H6
Distributed in the United Kingdom by GMC Distribution Services
Castle Place, 166 High Street, Lewes, East Sussex, England BN7 1XU
Distributed in Australia by Capricorn Link (Australia) Pty. Ltd.
P.O. Box 704, Windsor, NSW 2756, Australia

Manufactured in the United States of America
All rights reserved

Sterling ISBN 978-1-4027-7827-8

For information about custom editions, special sales, premium and
corporate purchases, please contact Sterling Special Sales
Department at 800–805–5489 or specialsales@sterlingpublishing.com.

Photographs of Ford Explorer provided courtesy of John Spangler.
http://www.johnspangler.com/

Contents

THE NEXT TIME

you want to post an ad

in the online classifieds, think again.

Somewhere out there, I am lurking,

just waiting for any signs of weakness to jump on.

It doesn't matter if you are

from Philadelphia or Boise, Idaho.

Wherever you are, if you post a stupid ad,

I will find you and take you down.

Automotive Sales

THE AUTOMOTIVE SECTION
of the classified ads is full of people looking for good, inexpensive cars. Some people even post ads demanding a free car. The ads are basically saying, "If you have a car lying around that you don't need anymore, I will gladly take it off your hands." Great! I thought I would never be able to get rid of that 2006 Escalade that is just taking up room in my driveway. It really amazes me that the people asking for a free car seem to think they can choose what kind of car they get. "I need a car to get to work, but I won't be seen in anything American or anything older than 1997." This is where I come in. I will show the victims just what kind of vehicle people are willing to give away for free. You don't want to pay more than $500 for a car? Well, you can have my Civic without a motor. It makes for a great mobile home.

On the flip side are the people who are trying to get way too much money for their shitty car. "Minor fender damage" really means "frame bent due to major collision." Why are there no pictures of the passenger side of the car? It most likely was hit by a train. Every time someone lists a car with high mileage, the miles are all highway miles, of course. These people expect thousands of dollars for a vehicle with a transmission that will die in a week. Hopefully I've helped discourage these people from ever selling a junk car online again.

The Shaniqua Chronicles

This was the ad that started it all. It had been six months since the transmission was ruined in my last car, and I had been constantly looking at ads for a lucky deal on a car. Then I came across this amazing ad, placed conveniently in the "for sale" section. **"HEY YOU THERE"**! How could I not click it?

Shaniqua's original ad:

******** **HEY YOU THERE** ******** $1500

HELLO I AM LOOKING FOR A FORD EXPLORER! I NEED A TRUCK SO IF YOU ARE SELLING YOURS AND IT HAS NO PROBLEMS WHAT SO EVER THEN LET ME KNOW. I'M A SINGLE MOTHER OF 3 BEAUTIFUL GIRLS AND WE NEED A WAY TO GET AROUND WHERE NO BODY WILL BE ALL CRAMPED UP AND A EXPLORER WILL DO US JUST FINE. I'M LOOKING TO BUY AROUND THE END OF OCTOBER IF YOU HAVE ONE THAT YOU WANT TO SELL THEN GET AT ME A.S.A.P.

Included with the ad was a picture of the lovely mother posing for the camera, as if someone would see her picture and realize that this woman had to have a car. The fact that this woman expected someone to give her a perfect car and that she thought she had a right to specifically demand a Ford Explorer made me realize that I couldn't let this ad go unanswered.

From Me to Shaniqua

Ay yo girl, i gots a Ford Explorer for you!

It's not really a 1997, it's a 1985 and it's not really a Ford Explorer, it's a Ford Bronco but it's like the same thing.

Here are the specs if you're interested:

- 217,292 miles.
- Transmission is in good shape, 5th gear and reverse work but the rest don't.
- The V6 engine was replaced with a V8, gas mileage is pretty good—I got about 12 mpg highway the other day but that was with premium.
- Power windows but you have to turn a crank to roll them down.
- Tape player—it does play but there is a Def Leppard tape jammed in there and it won't come out. Great for Def Leppard fans!
- I am a smoker so you can smell it in the car, but I'll throw in an air freshener for an extra 10 bucks.
- It came with front airbag, but it deployed in my last accident and I didn't get it replaced. Broncos are safe though so you won't have to worry about an airbag.
- The air conditioning does not work anymore, but it used to and was really cold.
- Heat works if you drive the car for a while.
- The frame is bent due to an accident with a tractor trailer, but as long as you don't drive over 40 you shouldn't have any problems.
- It can seat five which is good for kids, but the back seat has beer and urine stains. They have been professionally treated with Windex.
- The rear window is missing, but has been repaired with Saran Wrap.

- You will need to have some minor repairs done: new brakes, the rear axle is missing, needs a new radiator and coolant system. I spoke to my friend who knows a lot about cars and he said it shouldn't cost more than a few bucks.

I'm asking for $7,500 but am willing to negotiate.

Let me know what you think. —Ted

From Shaniqua to Me**:**

No thanks. That's not what I'm looking for it's too old and not even the right type of Ford. Have a nice day :)

From Me to Shaniqua**:**

I'm willing to drop the price to $7,000 and throw in a Phil Collins cassette tape for the tape player. Even though it may seem old, it still runs like it was OJ's Bronco. And don't worry about it not being an Explorer. All Fords are built Ford tough.

From Shaniqua to Me**:**

I don't think that you read my ad. I don't have $7000.00 to spend on a truck much less a DAMN 1985 BRONCO!!!!!!!!!!! You should be willing to give that old ass piece of shit away. GO AWAY and leave me the hell alone. STOP WASTING MY TIME!!!!!!!!!!!!!!!!!!!!

From Me to Shaniqua**:**

I see you are a tough negotiator. My final offer is $6,900, and I'll include a floor mat from my 1983 Cutlass Supreme. This floor mat is brown with several stains and cigarette burns, but it will keep the beautiful Bronco interior very clean. Please consider this generous offer.

From Shaniqua to Me**:**

READ THE AD—1500, THAT'S IT. I DON'T WANT YOUR DAMN FORD BRONCO!!!!!!!!!!!!!!!!!!!!!!!!!!!

From Me to Shaniqua:

Okay, I can see that this luxurious Bronco is out of your price range. That's okay. I have a cheaper car that you may be interested in.

It is a 1996 Geo Metro. Almost EXACTLY the same as a Ford Explorer. When looking at the two, I personally can't even tell the difference.

It was my son's car, but he lost his license after his third DUI, so now I am stuck with it. I have no use for it though and would be willing to sell it to you for $1550.

Features:

◆ 246,000 highway miles

◆ AM radio, great for traffic reports and radio Disney.

◆ 3 great tires from Walmart, they still have about 200 miles worth of tread on them.

◆ Partially functional transmission. Reverse does not work, but you don't really need that anyway.

◆ Due to a wheel alignment problem, the car can only turn right. But with power steering, it makes turning right easy. Three right turns can make a left.

◆ No title.

◆ Currently needs brakes, exhaust, cat converter, a front wheel and rotor, and a motor to pass inspection. But as long as you don't get pulled over, who cares about inspection?

◆ The paint is a metallic/rust red. Some of the spots have rusted through, but I covered them up with duct tape and spray paint. Looks good as new!

◆ Comes with THE CLUB, a state-of-the-art anti-theft device. But I lost the key to it, so it is stuck on the steering wheel. Great for leaving your car in west Philly!

◆ The gas tank currently leaks gas, so mpg is around 6 or 7

depending on how fast you drive. You just need to keep plugging the hole with gum.

At that price, this car is a DEAL! Let me know what you think.

From Shaniqua to Me:

YOU ARE AN ASSHOLE GO AWAY GO AWAY GO AWAY GET THE FUCK OUT OF MY FACE!!!!!!!!!!!!!!!!!

From Me to Shaniqua:

So you don't want the Geo? You're missing out on a dream car. Tell you what, for that price, I will also include three old Newsweek magazines, a used toaster, and an old Philadelphia Eagles #81 Terrell Owens jersey.

Anyone who is from Philadelphia knows how beloved a Terrell Owens jersey is. This woman just doesn't know value when she sees it.

I had so much fun fucking with her that I decided to make another email account and try to sell her another car. I just couldn't help myself.

From Me to Shaniqua:

Hey there! I saw your ad and I think I have the perfect car for you. I am selling my 2001 Ford Explorer Eddie Bauer edition. It is a great car and I hate to see it go, but I need the money to pay off my second DUI fines.

Only 72,000 miles! Here are the features:

- CD player
- Intact windshield
- Rear tires
- Spare tire

- New windshield wipers
- Beautiful white exterior paint
- Cloth interior

It was in a very MINOR fender bender, however, and will need a few repairs. As you can see from the picture, you may need to replace the passenger-side mirror and headlights in order for the car to pass PA inspection. I took it to a mechanic, and he said that the mirror is fixable.

I was selling the car for $1800, but due to these minor issues, I will drop the price to $1750.

Thanks,

Ryan Jackson

Attachment:

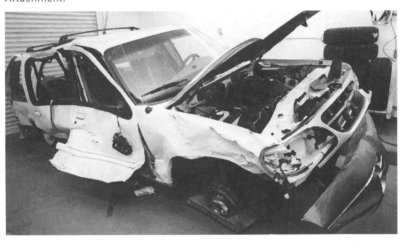

From Shaniqua to Me**:**

Hi I'm sorry I can't afford to buy your truck, it sounds really nice and I would love to be behind the wheel of it but I can't afford it. My budget will only allow for me to spend 1500, sorry

(She obviously didn't realize there was a picture.)

From Me to Shaniqua:

Tell you what, I'll bump the price down to 1500, but I get to keep the CD player and the passenger seat. And I will clear all of the change out of my ashtray.

This car is a great deal. I've included a picture, check it out and please reconsider!

From Shaniqua to Me:

WHY WOULD I BUT A PIECE OF JUNK WHY FOR WHAT YOU BETTA BET IT!!!!!!!!!!!!!!

Allow me to try and translate. I think she meant "Why would I buy a piece of junk, why? For what? You better beat it!"
Seeing how angry she got and imagining her yelling at her computer made me want to keep this up. I made yet another email account.

From Me to Shaniqua:

Hi there!

I saw your ad looking for a Ford Explorer. If it is not too late, please take a look at the one I am selling.

It's a 2000 Ford Explorer with 125,000 miles. It has always been a great car to me, but I recently upgraded to a 2001 Ford Explorer, so this thing has just been sitting in my backyard for the past few months. It looks almost brand-new! I am the original owner and took very good care of the car. It may need some MINOR paint work and possibly a rear tire.

$1500 is what I am asking.

I've attached a picture of it, let me know if you are interested. It has just been sitting in my backyard for a while, but I am pretty sure it still runs.

Thanks, John

Attachment:

From Shaniqua to Me**:**

ARE YOU FUCKIN SERIOUS THAT PIECE OF SHIT ISN'T WORTH $2.00. IF YOU DON'T GET THE FUCK OUTTA HERE WITH THAT SHIT!!!!!!!!!!!!!!!!!!!! WHAT DO YOU THINK THAT I'M FUCKIN STUPID? BET IT COCK SUCKER!!!!

Despite how angry she was, I wasn't quite ready to "BET IT" just yet. I made another email account and tried again. I was determined to put her behind the wheel of a lovely Ford Explorer.

From Me to Shaniqua**:**

Hello,

I saw your ad on ******** and I think I have a great car for you. I am selling my 1996 Ford Explorer. I used to work in the film industry, and I got this car after it was used in a movie. It has a custom paint job from the movie set. I barely drive it, so it has only around 60,000 miles on it. I really have no use for it anymore, so I am willing to get rid of it. Take a look at it and let me know what you think. I've attached a picture of it. Please note that it did have a MINOR accident involving an animal and may have slight damage.

Thanks!

Attachment:

From Shaniqua to Me:

Sir I thank you for trying to help but I don't want to drive the truck from the dinosaur movie. I wouldn't mind if I had money to get it painted over but I don't. Thanks anyway.

From Me to Shaniqua:

I always believe that you shouldn't judge a book by its cover, and you shouldn't judge this car by its paint job. It has a great engine that will not quit. From the inside, you can't even tell it is painted like that. This car is reliable and will NOT be going extinct any time soon.

From Shaniqua to Me:

No thanks!!!!

From Me to Shaniqua:

Tell you what, for an extra 50 bucks I will spray paint the entire car flat black. I took an art class in high school so I have some experience painting and it will look great.

From Shaniqua to Me:

NO THANKS!!! WHEN YOU GET A SHINY BLUE OR BLACK ONE THEN YOU LET ME KNOW.

From Me to Shaniqua:

Here's what I am willing to do. For $60, I will spray paint the entire car black, and then cover it with scotch tape so it is shiny. I'll also throw in a VHS of "Jurassic Park" I taped off of TBS 5 years ago. Includes many classic, retro commercials that you don't see on TV anymore. A collector's gold mine!

From Shaniqua to Me:

NO THANKS, TRY SOMEONE ELSE. I'VE ALREADY MADE A DEAL WITH SOMEONE ELSE, THEY WILL BE BRINGING ME THE TRUCK TOMORROW MORNING.

From Me to Shaniqua:

WAIT! Before you make that deal, check out the new, REPAINTED Explorer. I repainted it a nice shiny blue. Please check out the picture and reconsider!

Attachment:

What the hell is wrong with her? If someone tried to sell me that car, I would immediately tell them "fuck yes" and proudly drive it around every day. This woman just doesn't have good taste in movies.

That was the last time I ever heard from her. I guess she finally gathered enough common sense to stop replying to these emails. Just knowing that she had wasted her time reading all the emails and responding to them was enough satisfaction for me.

Camry Killer

selling 1997 toyota camry. 146k miles. engine and transmission in good shape. was in minor fender bender, damage shown in pictures

From Me to Derek:

Hello,

Let me just introduce myself. My name is Mike, and two weeks ago my dog was hit and killed by a car in Manayunk. The driver did not stop. He was hit by a white '97 Toyota Camry. With the side of the bumper bashed in like in your pictures. I thought I would never find the killer, but then I saw the murderer's car for sale in Manayunk! YOURS. What, are you trying to get rid of the evidence? You killed my dog of 8 years and didn't even stop. I had to tell my kids that they would never see him again. Now they just look dead inside, like their soul was taken from them. I can't blame them.

We can't bring Skip back to life, but I want you to come here and apologize to my kids. And buy them a new dog. It is the least you could do.

Email me back and we'll set up a time.

—Mike

From Derek to Me:

what? i didnt hit your fucking dog. no way im buying you a new dog

From Me to Derek:

There's no denying it. I've got you dead to rights. The car that hit my dog is unmistakably yours. I even remember seeing your Outer Banks bumper sticker as I watched the car drive away, leaving Skip in a mangled mess in the middle of the street.

Maybe you were drunk and didn't remember? That doesn't make you any less guilty.

From Derek to Me:

are you fucking serious i didnt hit your dog!!! i even called my girlfriend and she had no idea what i was talking about. you are mistaken

From Me to Derek:

No, I am not. Does your girlfriend have long hair? I didn't get a good look at the killer's face, but I saw long hair from behind as they sped away. I just assumed it was a man because of their huge shoulders.

From Derek to Me:

yes she has long hair but she didnt hit your dog. where did this happen?

From Me to Derek:

You know where it happened. Right here in Manayunk. I think your girlfriend is lying to you. I would like to meet both of you and have a good chat with you two so I can figure out which one of you is lying.

From Derek to Me:

no this is ridiculous neither of us hit your dog. im sorry it happened but this is not my fault

From Me to Derek:

Why would you be sorry if you didn't do it? Seems like you feel guilty about murdering my dog. Just own up to it. Do the right thing. For my kids.

I bet Derek and his girlfriend had a long talk about this. If he had reason to believe that she hit the dog, he probably still suspects her of it. I like how he just brushed off the comment about his girlfriend having huge shoulders. I guess I hit the nail on the head.

Barter My Whore Wife

Jim's original ad:

> i am looking to trade/barter my 1994 Jeep Wrangler.
> 140k miles, yellow, good condition. NO CASH. I will
> barter just about anything of equal value!

Jim said he would barter "just about anything." He is just setting himself up for strangers to suggest a bunch of random bullshit. I decided to take it a step further. I set up two email accounts for this one: Mike Anderson and Kira Anderson, the happily married couple. Mike, being the loving husband that he is, forwards every email to his wife.

From Mike Anderson to Jim:
CC: Kira Anderson:

Hey, I saw your ad for a '94 Wrangler for barter. I will trade you my whore of a wife for that car. She is a dirty little slut that fucks just about anything that moves. She doesn't really have much to offer, so I figure she is worth about the price of a used 1994 Wrangler. I understand if you think she isn't worth it, so I am willing to throw in $200 cash on top of that. If you are looking for a loose whore that will give it up easily, my wife will be well worth the trade. Let me know if you are interested. Does the Wrangler come with a title?

From Jim to Mike Anderson:

Ha ha! Very funny. I am married and don't think I would be interested in your wife. Thanks for the offer though!

From Kira Anderson to Mike Anderson and Jim:

OH FUCK YOU MIKE!! DROP FUCKING DEAD!!! YOU ARE SUCH A SCUMBAG PIECE OF SHIT I FUCKING HATE YOU!!!

From Mike Anderson to Kira Anderson and Jim:

Fuck YOU, you stupid cunt! What are you doing on the computer? I figured you were fucking Steve again. Or how about our neighbor? I'm sure he's looking to stick his dick in some rotten pussy.

From Kira Anderson to Mike Anderson and Jim:

MIKE YOU FUCKING ASSHOLE THIS IS IT. DONT EVEN THINK ABOUT COMING HOME TODAY BECAUSE I'LL BE WAITING WITH A FUCKIN KNIFE

From Mike Anderson to Kira Anderson and Jim:

Ooh I'm real fucking scared. It might be kind of hard to stab me with 10 inches of black dick in your mouth you fucking WHORE

From Jim to Mike Anderson and Kira Anderson:

Hey, you two sound like a great couple and all, but could you stop including me in these emails? I really don't think this concerns me.

From Kira Anderson to Jim and Mike Anderson:

TELL YOU WHAT, JIM, I'LL BUY YOUR FUCKING WRANGLER SO I CAN RUN OVER MY PIECE OF SHIT HUSBAND WITH IT

From Mike Anderson to Jim and Kira Anderson:

Jim, don't sell it to her. She'll probably pick up a random dude and crash the Jeep while she's sucking his dick.

From Kira Anderson to Jim and Mike Anderson:

FUCK YOU

From Jim to Mike Anderson and Kira Anderson:

Will both of you shut the fuck up and stop emailing me? Jesus fucking christ man c'mon!

Take that, Jim! I hope that will make you think twice about trying to barter your Wrangler. A Wrangler should only be bartered for badass manly shit anyway, like a shotgun or a mounted bear head.

Ford Camry

Alex's original ad:

> Looking for a cheap car that runs good, 1990s or newer.
> Preferably under 100,000 miles. Willing to pay up to $1500.

From Me to Alex:

Hey there!

I am trying to get rid of my son's '93 Ford Camry. 96,000 miles, you interested?

Mike

From Alex to Me:

That doesn't sound right. Are you sure you got the Make/Model right? Toyota makes the Camry.

From Me to Alex:

I know I got the make and model right. This is a rare vehicle from the Ford/Toyota merger in 1993. They merged on the 52th anniversary of the Pearl Harbor attacks, as a way to mend the tension that still existed between Japan and the US in the early nineties. They were only merged for several months, but managed to manufacture one of the finest vehicles on the road: The Ford Camry. If you don't want this classic car, I am sure there are plenty of others who will.

From Alex to Me:

I think you are full of shit. Is it a Toyota Camry or what?

From Me to Alex:

I assure you I am not lying. It is a Ford Camry. It is the luxurious Toyota Camry, except built Ford tough.

From Alex to Me:

Bullshit.

From Me to Alex:

What now?

(attachment):

From Alex to Me:

Shut up.

This guy thought he knew more about cars than I did. He didn't realize he was dealing with an expert on shitty cars from the '90s.

Free SUV

How could I not fuck with this person? She wants a free car, but you can forget it if you want to give her a brand-new convertible. It must be an SUV.

Laquita's original ad::

******* **I NEED A FREE CAR** *******

I WOULD LIKE AN SUV, IF YOU HAVE AN SUV IN GOOD SHAPE THAT YOU DONT WANT ANY MORE PLEASE CONTACT ME

From Me to Laquita:

Hi!

Do you still need a free car? I have a Jeep that I don't drive anymore. I hate selling things, so I'd gladly give it away.

Thanks, Mike

From Laquita to Me:

YES WHAT KIND OF JEEP IS IT? I ONLY WANT AN SUV

From Me to Laquita:

Laquita,

Luckily for you it isn't the sedan that Jeep makes. It is a 1997 Jeep Cherokee Sport. Here is everything about the car:

◆ 377,000 miles, but I assure you they are all either highway miles or off-roading miles.

Exterior damage:

- There is a dent in the side of my front passenger-side door from when a bum kicked it pretty hard. He was pissed off that I did not tip him for washing my windshield.

- The roof is dented in a little bit from when I tried to jump down to my car from my third-floor apartment balcony. You can't even tell if you are standing level with the car.

- There is this stain that appears to be bird shit on the back window, but no matter how hard I try, I can't seem to wash it off. I think the bird ate paint or something.

Interior damage:

- There are some cigar burns on the front seats.

- The ceiling caught on fire once when I accidentally lit a roman candle inside with all of the windows up. I managed to put out the fire with beer before it got out of control, but some of the ceiling is charred black. It looks kind of badass though.

- Sometimes the gas pedal will stick to the floor. The only way to unstick it is by crashing and putting the car in park. I put a new bumper on the front of the car in case this happens.

- I used to transport barrels of kitchen grease, and occasianally one would spill. The back of the car is lined with grease that will not wash out of the interior cloth. It isn't that bad though, and is actually very useful for items you do not want to be stuck in place as you are driving.

- One of my drunk friends jammed half of a grilled cheese sandwich into my tape deck. I managed to get most of the cheese out, but you can't play tapes now.

- The radio presets are set to a bunch of stations that suck. I don't know how to change them.

- There are footprints all over the ceiling, and it looks like the person stepped in tar or something. I don't know how it happened.

- The windshield is cracked from when I tried to de-ice my windshield with a cup of coffee.

I acquired the car from my friend after he went back to jail, so there are a lot of weird aftermarket parts. He doesn't have any of the paperwork, but if you want, I could try to guess the part numbers.

Would you like to come here and pick it up?

Thanks, Mike

From Laquita to Me:
FUCK YOU ASSHOLE I WANT A REAL SUV NOT A PEICE OF CRAP!

From Me to Laquita:
Laquita,

This is a real SUV. You are lucky I am giving this away for free. I've already had several inquiries about purchasing it from people who just happened to be passing by it. If you get the car detailed, it could end up being your dream car.

Oh, I almost forgot to mention that the engine needs a bit of work, particularly the transmission. Right now it does not have a working transmission, although the car still rolls down hills if you have it in neutral.

You will need to come pick it up and tow it or push it away, so bring a few friends if you plan on pushing it.

From Laquita to Me:
NO YOU GOD DAM FUCKIN SHIT HEAD MOTHER FUCKER FUCK YOU I WANT A STRATE UP RUNNING CAR

From Me to Laquita:
I assure you this car has all its paperwork in order. I was able to get some inspection stickers off of some other guy's car with a

heat gun and put them on mine. I am going to transfer the title to your name but I need some information from you, as well as $100.

From Laquita to Me:

I SAID FREE IM NOT PAYING SHIT YOU FUCKIN SCUMBAG

From Me to Laquita:

Laquita,

In that case, would you like some of my free car insurance and free gas as well? The car insurance will cover up to $25 in property damage or medical bills resulting from an accident. The gas is two cans of torch fluid but may be able to power a vehicle.

Thanks,

Mike

Suddenly I'm the asshole for trying to help this woman out.

Employment
Opportunities

THE JOB EMPLOYMENT SECTION
of the classified ads is one of my favorites. Who
is going to hire someone who wants to be a "desk
resepsonist"? A desk receptionist who lacks the
ability to spell is a must-have for every office. There
are also people who think that they will be getting good and cheap
labor by hiring someone off the internet. When I write to them,
I show them that this is not the case. The job employment section
usually has two types of ads that are equally fun to mess with.

The first type of ad is posted by people looking to hire someone
for a quick job, such as fixing a sink or mowing a lawn. I never
understand why people are so lazy that they will put an ad online
saying "I need a plumber" when they could simply look up the
phone number of a plumber and call. Some people put ads online
specifying what they are willing to pay—ads like "I want you to
do my roof, and I only want to pay $20 for it." I like to show these
people exactly what they get when they pay for really cheap labor.
I play the role of the common man simply trying to get a job—
with a catch. Maybe I suck at what I do. Maybe I come off as a
complete lunatic. Or maybe I am simply an asshole.

Then there are people looking for jobs. I like to put these
people to the test, to see how much shit they will actually put up

with for money. You are looking for a summer job? How about brutally murdering animals all day for pay? Oh, you want to be a model? How much will it cost to take pictures of you up to your neck in cow shit? Some victims refuse to break their principles, while others will do just about anything for the right price.

Discount Limos

I remember I wanted to have a Hummer limo drop me off in front of my high school to piss off the members of the environmental club, but my idea was quickly shot down when I found out how expensive it was to rent a limo. This woman thinks she can go online and just beg for a limo, so I decided to show her what she could get for the money.

Diana's original ad:

> We need a limousine for about eight hours on the day of our wedding (June 7, 2010). We don't have much money, so we are looking for something cheap (around $500 maybe?) Please contact with rates and photos. Thank you.

From Me to Diana:

I saw your ad looking for a limousine service and would like to help you. I run a limousine service with a large variety of vehicles and rates. Let me know if you are interested and we can discuss further details.

Thank you.

Michael Partlow

Founder

Partlow Limousines

From Diana to Me:

Mr. Partlow,

Thank you for your response! I still need a limo and we will have 7 people including myself in the limo. Can you send your rates and a photo of the limo?

Best,

Diana

From Me to Diana:

Diana,

Since you have 7 people, I recommend my SUV limousine so all of you can ride in luxury on your important day. I'll put you with one of my best drivers. His rate is $60 per hour, so for 8 hours it would cost you $480. I've included a picture of it for you.

Michael

Attachment :

From Diana to Me:

What the fuck is that?

From Me to Diana:

It is our luxurious Jeep Cherokee limousine. It is a classic 1996 model that can seat 7 comfortably when the seat in the back is folded down. I'm going to book you with Jim; he is a very nice driver who will get you wherever you want to go fast and safe.

From Diana to Me:

I want a real limo, not a fucking Jeep! Who pays $60 an hour to get driven around in some piece of shit Jeep caked in fucking dirt?

From Me to Diana:

Diana,

I assure you that is a real limo. That picture is a few weeks old. It has rained since then and a lot of the dirt has washed off. Trust me, it doesn't get much better for the price! If you want something nicer, though, here are our vehicles and their respective rates:

1987 Ford Bronco—$45/hr

1992 Toyota Camry—$50/hr

1996 Jeep Cherokee—$60/hr

1975 Chrysler New Yorker—$70/hr

1993 Geo Metro—$80/hr

I would like to point out that the Geo Metro has a classy spoiler and racing stripes, as well as an aftermarket muffler.

We also have a driver who will drive you for 30% off the advertised rate. He doesn't have a license because of a vehicular manslaughter conviction, but it wasn't really his fault. The pedestrians he hit shouldn't have been on the sidewalk in the first place. I assure you he is still a great driver.

Let me know if you are interested in any of the other vehicles. I believe the Bronco is the only one we have booked for that date.

Michael

From Diana to Me:

How the fuck do you get any business with those piece of shit cars you are trying to pass off as limos! What a joke!

From Me to Diana:

We have plenty of business with our affordable limos. Sorry if it isn't the diamond-covered Bentley you were expecting to get for $500. Why don't you allocate your wedding budget better? I suggest pawning your engagement ring if you want a better limo. They say you can always get a new engagement ring, but you have only one chance to experience an unforgettable limo ride. Go big or go home!

I was a little bit offended that she thought that Jeep was a piece of shit. That is actually a picture I took of my beloved Jeep—the only car that I own. As you can see, I take excellent care of it.

My Son's Birthday

Susan's original ad:

Is your child having a birthday party? Look no further! We will take care of everything you need for your child's birthday party. For $100, our package will be mailed to you with everything you need (hats, plates, balloons, etc.) We could even order a custom-made cake. Put your child's party in the hands of professionals. Contact us at ********@gmail.com.

From Me to Susan:

Hi there,

My son Stephen is turning seven years old next month, and I want to throw him a big party. Your birthday party package seems like it could save me a lot of time. I have a few more things I need though, and I was wondering if you would be able to help me out.

Thanks,

Mike

From Susan to Me:

Hello Mike. Thank you for your interest in our birthday package. When is the date of the party and what else do you need? Here is what comes in a standard package:

- 12 party hats
- 24 paper plates
- 1 bag of balloons

- **2 rolls of streamers**
- **1 pack of candles**
- **1 pack of confetti**
- **12 party gift bags (containing small toys)**

Thank you,

Susan

From Me to Susan:

Susan, I will need all of those things, as well as alcohol and erotic dancers. I am thinking maybe some single malt scotch for me, and some light beer for the kids. My son likes to watch "Bob the Builder," so please find a stripper who could dress up as Wendy, Bob's business partner in the show. She could just wear a generic construction worker outfit when she shows up. I am willing to pay a little more than your $100 package in exchange for these extra items. I'd find them myself, but I am banned from calling the stripper place that I usually call, and I am under house arrest for a nonviolent crime so I can't go out to get the booze.

Thanks again for your help!

Mike

From Susan to Me:

Are you the sole guardian for your son? I hope to God you're not. What you want to do is illegal and wrong in so many ways (ever hear of serving alcohol to a minor?) I can sell you the standard package but nothing else!

From Me to Susan:

Well, my ex-girlfriend (his mother) is in jail for violating her parole. So I guess that makes me the sole guardian, although before I was on house arrest, when I would go to Atlantic City I would just let my son guard himself with my .357 Magnum.

I'm not quite sure I get the point of your email. Is it going to be a problem to get these things? I forgot to ask, would you be able to pick up a carton of menthol cigarettes for me as well? You can substitute this for the birthday candles. We usually just stick lit cigarettes in the birthday cake. My son likes them because they remind him of his mother, who used to smoke menthols.

From Susan to Me:

Your son should be taken away from you by social services!

From Me to Susan:

Susan, when you go and say something like that, it makes me not want to give you my address. Sorry, Susan, but you just lost yourself a customer.

This woman thought she could get $100 for a bunch of shit I could find at a party store for $10. If she really wants to get business, she is going to have to learn that birthday parties are only fun with strippers and alcohol.

A Walk to Remember

> We're currently looking for artists who own a drawing tablet and are skilled in the art of sequential storytelling. We have a large number of scripts that we need to have storyboarded ASAP. We will provide the script and storyboarding template. You will develop the storyboards for the scenes, adding notes to the template when needed.
>
> Please send us samples of your work and/or links to your online portfolio, etc.

I have always prided myself on my artistic talent, so I thought I would be perfect for this ad.

From Me to Pete:

Hello,

I am a professional storyboard artist and happened to come across your ad. I've attached my most recent storyboard I did for a short piece called "A Walk to Remember."

Thanks,

Mike

Attachment:

From Pete to Me:

That's an interesting piece of art. Did "A Walk to Remember" get produced as a finished video?

Pete

From Me to Pete**:**

Yes, it actually won several awards at a film festival last year. I was nominated for best storyboard but lost to someone else.

From Me to Pete**:**

Pete,

Just a follow-up. Are you interested in my services as a story-boarder?

Mike

I never heard back from Pete, which is a damn shame. I could have done wonders with his scripts.

Horse Farm

Stephanie's original ad:

> I am a 18 year old looking for a summer job.
> it is hard for me to find work and I just want a
> job so I can afford a car for college next summer.
> I can clean, babysit, answer phones, pretty much
> whatever as long as it pays!!

From Me to Stephanie:

Hey,

I saw your ad looking for work and I think I have a job for you! I am looking for an assistant on my farm for the summer. It will involve working outdoors. Let me know if you are interested.

Mike

From Stephanie to Me:

Hi Mike! I am interested in your job! I love animals and used to ride horses so a farm would be great! what kind of work would I be doing, and where is your farm located? it needs to be close to ****** so my parents can drop me off and pick me up.**

From Me to Stephanie:

Stephanie,

It is very close to ********. I'm glad to hear you are familiar with horses, because you will be primarily working with horses.

My farm gets all the old horses that other farms don't need

anymore, and they are starting to take up a lot of room in my stable, which I want to turn into a garage for my new truck. Therefore, the horses need to go. As my assistant, you will be in charge of killing the horses and dumping them in the lake behind my farm.

I used to have a captive bolt pistol (cattle gun) that I used to put them down, but it broke when I tried to use it to tap a keg. You'll probably have to use my 12-gauge shotgun to put them down. Sometimes they don't die right away when you shoot them and will start freaking out. You just have to stay calm and keep shooting. Don't worry, I'll show you how to use the shotgun if you aren't familiar with one.

You then need to use my chainsaw to cut the horses into smaller parts that you can carry down to the lake. It can get a little messy, so I suggest wearing clothes that you don't care about or an outfit that the horse blood would complement.

The lake isn't mine, it is my neighbor's. He gets kind of angry when he sees me dumping dead horses in his lake, so you have to make sure he isn't around when you do it. I have some cinder blocks you can use to weigh the horses down so he won't see them.

I have a lot of horses, and each horse takes about an hour and a half to dispose of, so you should have plenty of work. The job will pay $15 an hour. When can you start?

Mike

From Stephanie to Me:

omg that is HORRIBLE! That is truely awful and sick!! Why cant you just give the poor horses away? sorry but I am not helping you slaughter horses!!!

From Me to Stephanie:

Stephanie,

I'm sorry if you are a bit surprised, but this is how farms work. You can't give away old horses, you have to kill them. I thought about it, and if you don't want to use the chainsaw to cut up the horses, you can just use my truck to drag them down to the lake. Do you have your license or permit? If not, this could be good driving practice for you. You don't want to pass up on this great job opportunity.

Mike

From Stephanie to Me:

No that is not how farms work, you are just SICK! I am NOT interested

From Me to Stephanie:

Stephanie, you are going to regret this some day when you try to get a real job. I think this would look great on your resume.

I didn't quite know where this email was going to go when I contacted Stephanie. Once I read that she loved horses, however, I knew I had the perfect job for her. At least I thought so. What an ungrateful bitch. Girls really hate it when you talk about horses dying. I had a friend who loved her pet horse, and I always joked about it getting run over by an industrial mulching machine. She was not amused.

It really would have looked great on Stephanie's resume when she went to get a real job some day. "Let's see . . . it says here you used to murder and dismember horses and dispose of them in a lake. Great! We will fast-track you to upper management."

I don't think Stephanie will ever look at a horse farm the same way again.

Excellent Job Reference

If I'm browsing the ads and come across an ad printed in all capital letters, it is a big flag for me. It usually indicates that the person writing the ad is "new to this whole computer thing" and, most likely, an idiot. These people seem to expect that because they're posting their ad on the internet, they will get serious replies. I didn't know exactly where this conversation was headed at first, but I figured I'd come up with something if he replied.

Eric's original ad:

> I HAVE SEVERAL OUTLETS IN MY HOUSE THAT DO NOT WORK. LOOKING FOR EXPERIENCED ELECTRICIAN. MUST HAVE REFERENCES.

From Me to Eric:

I am a very experienced electrician and will be able to fix your outlets for an affordable price. I have several references if you need them.

Thanks, Mike

From Eric to Me:

YES MIKE PLEASE SEND ME A REFERENCE OR TWO. THANKS.

From Me to Eric:

Okay, I'm going to give you the contact information for Jim Roberts, who I did some electrical work for recently. His email address is ********@gmail.com.

This just goes to show how easy it is to fake a job reference.
All I had to do was create an email account for Jim Roberts . . .

From Eric to Jim Roberts:

HI JIM I WAS REFERRED TO YOU BY MIKE PARTLOW. I AM CONSIDERING HIRING MIKE TO DO SOME ELECTRICAL WORK ON MY HOUSE AND WANTED TO KNOW IF HE IS RELIABLE. THANKS.

From Jim Roberts to Eric:

Mike Partlow? Yeah, I remember him. My wife and I hired him to fix a faulty outlet in our basement about five months ago. At first, we thought he had fixed it. But then we realized that he actually just ran an extension cord from another outlet to behind this outlet and taped it up to the plug so it looked like it worked. Really shoddy work. When we called him and demanded our money back, he apologized and said that he was on a lot of horse tranquilizers that day, and he offered to fix it for free. I'm not sure what he did, but when I went down to the basement to check on him I think I caught him putting out a fire on the back of our couch. He then asked me if "that bitch" that I'm living with was single and "down to fuck." I asked him to leave, but I'm pretty sure that while he was down there he stole my daughter's Dora the Explorer DVDs and tried to bite a piece of fake fruit we had on display. Our wooden apple clearly had bite marks in it. So I guess what I'm saying is, don't hire this asshole.

From Eric to Jim Roberts:

WOW HE SOUNDS LIKE A RETARD! THANKS FOR SAVING ME MY TIME AND MONEY.

To my surprise, I didn't hear back from Eric.
I had to make sure he was still interested.

From Mike Partlow to Eric:

Hey Eric, I was just wondering if you got in contact with Jim yet. I am really looking forward to starting work with you.

From Eric to Mike Partlow:

YEAH, HE SAID YOU DID SHITTY WORK AND YOU STOLE FROM HIM. DONT THINK I'M GONNA BE HIRING YOU.

From Mike Partlow to Eric:

What? He's fucking lying! I did outstanding work and I didn't steal shit. I know where that asshole lives, I'm gonna go kick his ass. Let me see if I can find another reference that isn't a fucking liar.

From Eric to Mike Partlow:

THAT WONT BE NECESSARY BECAUSE I'M NOT HIRING YOU.

From Mike Partlow to Eric:

You just wait. We'll see what Jim has to say about me after I'm done kicking his ass up and down his professionally wired house.

From Jim Roberts to Eric:

Hey Eric! I just remembered, I was mistaken about all of those things I said about Mike Partlow. I had him confused with this crackhead that broke into our basement. Mike is a great electrician and you should definitely hire him.

From Eric to Jim Roberts:

DID MIKE JUST COME OVER THERE AND YELL AT YOU?

From Jim Roberts to Eric:

What? Of course not. Please hire him.

From Eric to Jim Roberts:

NO

From Jim Roberts to Eric:

Please! Just hire him. I'll hire him for you! Please just let him work on your house. I'm begging you.

I hope you feel guilty, Eric.
Your big mouth made Jim Roberts get his ass kicked.

Children's Storyteller

Beth's original ad:

> I'm looking for a friendly, entertaining storyteller
> to tell stories to children at an afternoon party on
> Halloween. I need you to tell stories for about an
> hour or so. Compensation is $40.

From Me to Beth:

Hello,

I am writing in response to your ad looking for a kid's storyteller for your Halloween party. I have a lot of great, scary stories that children love. If you are still looking for a storyteller, I am your man.

Thanks,

Mike

From Beth to Me:

Hi Mike!

I do need a storyteller! I am having a party for all the neighborhood kids that starts around 4 pm and will last until everyone is ready to trick-or-treat. I only need you to tell stories for about an hour. Most of the kids are five to ten years old, so the stories should be scary, but appropriate. I will pay you $40 for the hour and you can help yourself to any food or drinks. Do you think you have enough stories to entertain children for a whole hour?

Beth

From Me to Beth:

I absolutely have plenty of stories to tell. I did three tours of 'Nam and have a ton of stories about it. $40 is reasonable compensation. What kind of drinks do you have? I am a scotch man, so if you have at least 20-year-old single malt Glenfiddich, that would be great.

From Beth to Me:

I want you to tell the kids Halloween stories, not war stories. (For example, the headless horseman, ghost/goblin stories, etc.) Can you tell any of those? Seeing as it is a children's party, I won't be serving scotch, rather soda and juice.

From Me to Beth:

Not a problem. I have just the story for your party; my grandchildren love it. It's called "The Headless VC," and it took place on October 31st, 1970. I'll go into more details at your party, but to give you the gist of it, our squad was sent out on a patrol late on Halloween eve. It was seemingly normal until we came under heavy RPG fire. Walked right into a fucking ambush. Enemy small arms fire was tearing us to shreds. The guy next to me got his leg ripped off by an RPG explosion. The fucking thing landed right on my lap, covered in blood. Before I knew it, Charlie was right on top of me. He was charging me with his bayonet, so I had to act fast. Figures, my fucking M16 jammed on me. I looked around and grabbed the first thing I could find, which happened to be an M-79 grenade launcher covered in blood. By the time I grabbed it, the Charlie was two feet away from me. I took the M-79 and put a 40mm round right through his fucking head. It ripped his head clean off, spraying blood everywhere. To my astonishment, even without a fucking head, the VC kept running for another ten feet before falling to the ground. I guess it was some weird nerve reaction from getting his head blown clean off, kind of like when you cut a snake in half and it keeps slithering. And that is the story of "The Headless VC."

I have a couple of other stories you can choose from for me to tell. Here is a brief summary of each:

◆ The first time I slit a VC's throat. A really exhilarating story.

◆ The time I got shot in the leg and had to pull the bullet out with my bare hands.

◆ The time one of my men blew up a hut full of Charlie with a white phosphorus grenade.

◆ The time I accidentally blew a horse to pieces with a claymore mine.

I'll probably only have time to tell two or three of those stories. My grandkids love the story about the white phosphorus grenade. It really is amazing how that shit burns through flesh, straight to the bone.

Let me know which stories you want, and I'll practice them before I come over.

Thanks,

Mike

From Beth to Me:

Mike, thanks but no thanks. That story is waaaaaaaaaay too profane and graphic even for my tastes. I don't know how old your grandkids are but those stories would surely traumatize the children at my party!

From Me to Beth:

Beth,

My grandkids are five and seven, and they have no problem with these stories. I didn't realize the children at your party were a bunch of pussies. If they can't deal with a fun little war story, then I don't think they are being raised properly. If you want, I can bring over my service pistol from the war. It is a .45 Colt 1911. That'll put some hair on their chests. I'll let the boys shoot it off in the backyard or basement if you have one. I also have a Makarov that I got off a dead VC officer, which I will let the girls shoot. I've found that girls suck at shooting guns, but the Makarov is a smaller caliber than the 1911 so they shouldn't have a problem with it. That reminds me—I have a funny story about how that officer died that I could tell the kids.

Now, ammo ain't cheap, especially with all that talk about harsher gun laws and shit. If you give me an extra $30, I can get a box of 100 rounds for the .45.

Looking forward to meeting you,

Mike

From Beth to Me:

You're delusional!! I thought I was clear before but let me repeat myself. I don't want you at my party!

> One of my favorite things to do is to show parents that they really shouldn't be looking on the internet for people to deal with their children. Hopefully, this woman will think twice before saying "I'll just look on the internet for a complete stranger to hang out with my children for an hour!"
>
> If I were the parent, however, I would have jumped on the opportunity to have a badass Vietnam veteran tell stories and traumatize the neighborhood kids. The neighbors would probably never ask me to host a party again.

Tyrone's Dog-Sitting Service

Tanya's original ad:

> DOG WATCHER WANTED! we are leaving town for a week and need someone to take care of our 6-year-old rottweiler. he is very friendly! we are looking for someone trustworthy with experience, so we will need references. will pay $30 per day. email if interested!

From Me to Tanya:

yo wat up! i saw your ad looking for someone to take care of your rottweiler. i'll do it, no problem. i live in the area and can pick him up.

Tyrone Jackson

From Tanya to Me:

tyrone, do you have any references? can you tell us a little about yourself?

From Me to Tanya:

yeah i got some references. you can talk to my bro devon, or my associate g-ice. i'll have them hit u up. a little about myself: i love taking care of dogs and shit.

now you said your rottweiler is friendly. how friendly is he? would he be able to fight another dog if they were both put in a ring? just wonderin.

also can you pay me the money up front straight cash? i need it to enter in a contest.

From Tanya to Me:

I don't want you watching my dog!!!! find someone else for your dog-fighting ring, sicko!!!!!!!

From Me to Tanya:

whoa whoa slow yo role! who said anything about dog fighting? i was just wondering if your dog could protect itself, in case an angrier dog tries to start some shit while i'm walkin him. you need to chill the fuck out and stop jumpin to conclusions.

From Me to Tanya:

look, you triflin bitch, just gimme the dog. i need it, the fight is tonight! i'll pay you 200 cash plus 20 percent of whatever i win.

From Tanya to Me:

STOP IT

A few hours later I emailed her again from
another account as Tyrone's "associate" G-Ice.

From Me to Tanya:

ay yo wat up, woman, its ya boy, tyrone's boy G-Ice. tyrone was sayin he needed a reference for ur dog babysittin job so here i am. tyrone be great with dogs. he loves em so much and will care the shit out of em. my boy tyrone is definitely the right man for the job, i aint playin.

From Tanya to Me:

GO AWAY

Thanks to this bitch, I had to settle for a French poodle
and lost $200 that night.

Didgeridon't Join Our Band

Ads looking for musicians are particularly fun for me to mess with, but hard to put on paper. I usually record an amazingly terrible song as my sample hit single and then watch as the people I am emailing struggle to be polite and tell me that I am simply not what they are looking for. This guy did not even need to hear a sample, though.

Kyle's original ad:

SINGER/LYRICAL WRITER WANTED

we are a death metal/hardcore band looking for the right singer. we have two guitarists, a bassist, and a drummer. we write original songs and have a lot of metal influences. contact us to set up an audition.

From Me to Kyle**:**

G'day!

My name is Jack Walker and I saw your ad looking for a singer for your band. While I do not sing, I am a classically trained didgeridoo player. I recently moved here from Australia, where I was in a very popular Aborigines band. If you want, we can meet up and I'll jam out on the didgeridoo for you.

Let me know if you are interested, mate.

Cheers!

Jack

From Kyle to Me:

what the hell is a didgeridoo

From Me to Kyle:

Mate, if you do not know what a didgeridoo is, I suggest you Google it. It will be the perfect addition to your band.

Jack

From Kyle to Me:

that is RETARDED! we are looking for a death metal singer, not some boomerang throwing kangaroo jack motherfucker

From Me to Kyle:

Kyle,

I can play all styles of music on the didgeridoo, including death metal. You won't even need a singer—the rich tones of my didgeridoo are more hardcore than anything a singer can do. Most metal bands have a didgeridoo player anyway.

P.S. Although I am a boomerang enthusiast, not all Australians throw boomerangs, ride kangaroos, and "put shrimp on the barbie." You shouldn't be so naive.

Jack

From Kyle to Me:

whatever, dude. we dont need your fuckin didgeridoo skills but thanks

I personally think a didgeridoo would make an awesome addition to any band, but metal elitists are so picky about their music that I guess they aren't open to any new things.

Handicapped Movers

I am looking for help moving on June 23rd into my new apartment. We will need to load everything from my old apartment into a truck and then drive to my new place and unload it. I have a lot of furniture that is very heavy, as well as a big-screen tv that is bulky. We will need to lift a lot of this stuff down three flights of stairs since it won't fit in my elevator. I will pay $25/hr.

From Me to Jerry:

Good afternoon!

I saw your ad asking for help moving your furniture into your new apartment. I was wondering if you would be interested in hiring my son. I need him to have a job like this so he can feel better about himself. He has been paralyzed from the neck down for five years now. I always encourage him to do normal things like mow the lawn, take out the trash, etc., so he can still feel important even though he does not have the use of his arms or legs. This job would be a huge boost in his self-esteem and with a little help I am sure he can do it. Please consider him!

Mike

From Jerry to Me:

Mike,

I'm sorry, but I don't think this job would be appropriate for your son. A lot of the stuff I need to move is very large and heavy. He sounds like a good kid, but I don't think he would be able to do this. Thanks for the offer, though.

Jerry

From Me to Jerry:

Jerry,

I think you are underestimating my son. He can do anything he puts his mind to. I told him I got him a job and he was so excited. Do I really have to tell him now that the guy changed his mind because he hates handicapped people?

Mike

From Jerry to Me:

Oh man . . .

I don't hate handicapped people. I just don't see how your son can help, no offense. How can he move anything with his arms and legs? You said he mows the lawn and takes out the trash, how is that even possible?

I apologize, but next time you shouldn't tell your son you got him a job before making sure it is okay with the employer.

Jerry

From Me to Jerry:

Jerry,

Don't tell me how to raise my son. You don't see me telling you how to move your furniture, do you? You never even met my son, and already you are telling me what he can and can't do. He does a great job mowing the lawn. We tie the lawn mower to the back of his wheelchair and he drags it around. You'd be surprised how much torque that wheelchair has. It makes him feel normal again.

I don't have the heart to tell him that he won't be doing this job, so would you be able to come over here and tell him yourself that you hate him and will not hire him? It is the least you could do.

Mike

From Jerry to Me:

You've got to be kidding me. This conversation is over.

This guy tried to be polite, but in return I tried to shit all over his politeness. If he had agreed to do this, I might have felt bad. I would have showed up for the job and said, "Your kindness showed me that anything is possible, and I can walk again!" I wouldn't have helped move the furniture, though.

Tour Manager

From Me to James:

Hello,

My name is Mike, and I want to be your manager. I am ready to move up in life, and I think I have what it takes to be a full-time tour manager. Now I don't have much experience in this field. My last five years were spent working at Blockbuster. But in that time, I have watched plenty of movies about bands that go on tour. I have seen "Spinal Tap" and regularly play "Guitar Hero: World Tour," so I am familiar with the tricks of the trade. The service I offer is invaluable. You will not regret hiring me.

Thanks,

Mike

From James to Me:

Dear Mike:

Please let me know a little bit more about you and what your goals are in the field of entertainment. I am looking to work with dedicated, driven, and organized people. I have a lot of things going on right now and would love to hear more about you. Thanks for your time.

Sincerely,

James and ******** Entertainment

From Me to James:

James,

My goals in entertainment are to become a successful tour manager and live a life of drugs, sex, and rock and roll. I want to have sex with a different girl every night on tour and do massive amounts of cocaine. I hope you consider me for your manager position.

Thanks,

Mike

From James to Me:

Dear Mike:

I thank you for your interest in the management position, but these are not qualities that I look for in any manager, agent, or anyone that I work with. I hope that you do well and I once again thank you for your time.

Sincerely,

James and ******** Entertainment

From Me to James:

James,

You obviously do not know what rock and roll is really about. When you are done touring with the Backstreet Boys and Jonas Brothers, hit me up for a real tour.

Mike

This must have been a quality pop artist and actor if he was still considering me after I told him my only experience was working at Blockbuster for the last five years. If this guy ever does make it big, he is going to realize that being famous is about banging as many chicks as possible and doing as much coke as possible. Then, hopefully, he will fire whatever straight-edge, politically correct manager he has hired and come crawling back to me.

Pest Control

It has always been my dream to make a living by hunting. One time while I was shopping in a supermarket, I noticed a bunch of birds flying around. I offered to take care of the birds if the manager gave me $100 and left me alone in the store all night with a BB gun. To my disappointment, the manager wouldn't hire me and my dream was crushed. That is, until I found this ad.

Megan's original ad:

I have several groundhogs living under my shed that I need removed due to the damage they cause to my garden. If you are an expert at trapping/removing small animals, please contact me.

From Me to Megan:

Hello,

I am writing in response to your ad looking for help in disposing of some problem animals. If you still wish to employ a professional, please let me know.

Thank you,

Mike

From Megan to Me:

Dear Mike,

I still am looking for someone to do this, yes. You are the only

person who responded. I have seen at least 3 different groundhogs living under the shed but there might be even more. What will it cost to get rid of them?

Megan

From Me to Megan:

Megan,

It depends on the method you would like me to use to remove the animals. Generally, for this situation I would recommend using claymores to dispose of them. I would set the trap and then leave, and you should see results in a day or two. This will cost you about $150. Other methods require me being on your property until I catch the groundhogs, for which I'd charge a rate of $50 an hour until I neutralize all the targets.

Let me know what you want to do.

Thanks,

Mike

From Megan to Me:

Mike,

What are claymores? Isn't that a sword?

Megan

From Me to Megan:

Megan,

No, I meant claymore mines. Claymore mines are directional mines that have a small plastic explosive in them and contain steel ball bearings that are sent flying toward the groundhog's direction when the explosive is detonated. What I would do is set a trip-wire by the entrance to the groundhog's hole and then direct the mine toward the entrance of the hole. Any groundhog coming out of the hole will be shredded into a thousand pieces.

Do you have any children or pets? If so, I recommend you keep them inside so they don't accidentally set off the mine.

From Megan to Me:

Um, isn't that a little extreme? I thought you were going to trap them with a conventional rodent trap. I have neighbors and don't think they would appreciate someone setting off explosives in their neighborhood. What other methods do you have?

From Me to Megan:

My methods are extreme, but effective. From what you described, it sounds like we are dealing with hardened veteran groundhogs that will stop at nothing to cripple your garden. I just want to bring all the right tools to the fight. Although the claymore explosions are not that loud, I'll understand if you don't want me to use them.

The next option I offer is for me to set up a sniper position in your backyard and wait until the groundhogs come out to shoot them. Do you have any trees or bushes that I would be able to set up in? I would wear a ghillie suit and bring a spotter who will also be wearing a ghillie suit. The most important thing for a sniper is patience, so we will wait as long as it takes to get the perfect shot on the groundhogs. Some jobs can take up to a week, at $50 an hour. I will not sleep and will have a limited supply of food. During this time, I will ask that you do not come out and talk to me so that you do not compromise my position.

Now I would prefer to use a .50-caliber Barrett M82 sniper rifle to ensure that the groundhog is killed, but it is a very loud weapon. I know you have issues with noise, so I can use a Springfield M1A with a silencer and subsonic ammunition. The M1A has a smaller caliber bullet (.308) but should be able to kill the groundhogs, and none of the neighbors will see or hear it. My spotter and I will be ghosts; nobody will know that we are there.

This is a more expensive option, but I assure you it is very effective.

Let me know when you decide to green-light the operation and we will be there within 20 minutes.

From Megan to Me:

Are you ex-military? I think you are a bit delusional. I just want traps. Traps. Got it? Traps for small animals. No bombs, no guns, none of your crazy army missions, just come and trap the animals and leave. Can you do that?

From Me to Megan:

I am not at liberty to discuss that matter, but I will tell you that I used to be part of a very elite animal extermination task force that has assassinated high-priority animals all over the world. I am the best at what I do, and if you want the job done right, you will let me do my job the way I want to.

These groundhogs are no joke. You can't simply catch them with a trap; they are smarter than that. The only way to stop them is with firepower. I have already briefed my spotter on the mission and he is ready to roll. Just give us the green light and we will be on the move.

From Megan to Me:

I didn't tell you to do that, you jackass. I've made a mistake trying to find a sane person on the internet. I'm giving up and putting cayenne pepper on my plants like I always do. Thanks for nothing.

If she had said yes at any time in this conversation, I actually would have gone over to her house and trapped those groundhogs. I would have even bought a ghillie suit for it—that is how excited I would have been.

Very Strong Dog Walker

This ad struck me as odd. He is looking for a "verry strong" person to walk his dog because no average person would be able to handle a Doberman. I just pictured a giant bodybuilder jumping on the opportunity.

Original ad:

> ## WALK MY DOG
>
> walkn my dog for excdercise , must be verry strong person he is a docile but strong doberman friendly , please be local only , respond with your information, thanks

From ME to ********:

HI THERE,

MY NAME IS MAGNUS. I AM VERY STRONG PERSON. YOUR DOG SOUNDS LIKE A GOOD CHALLENGE FOR EXERCISE. HOW MUCH DOES DOG WEIGH?

MAGNUS KRISTUELSON

From ****** to Me:

magnus that is your name that tells me nothing about you or your experience at all reply with location and other information or dont reply at all and waste my time , i have had dozens of responses.

From ME to ********:

MAGNUS SHOULD BE ALL THE INFORMATION YOU NEED. WITH A NAME LIKE MAGNUS, YOU HAVE TO BE STRONG AND POWERFUL. I AM VERY EXPERIENCED WITH HEAVY OBJECTS. YOUR PUNY MUTT IS NO MATCH FOR MY STRENGTH.

From ******** to Me:

pleasae do not e mail me again

Strong people have to type in all capital letters to show how hard they are pounding the keyboard.

Comatose Grandma Sitter

From ME to ********:

Hey,

I saw your ad about babysitting and am very interested. My grand-mother is in the hospital and is probably going to die. She is never awake when I am there, and the doctors say she is only awake for about 5 minutes every couple of days. The problem is, I need her to sign a re-drafted will I wrote so I can get all her stuff when she dies. Right now she has all her money going to my bitch sister and her family. I don't have the time to sit there and watch her all day because I have better things to do. I need you to sit at the hospital and watch her in case she wakes up, and then you can make her sign the will. I will pay you $10 an hour for this job.

Thanks,

Tim

From ******** to Me:

no thanks, that is sick! show some sympathy, you prick!

From ME to *********:

Obviously I am not offering you enough money. I will pay you $15 an hour, but in return I need you to unplug her life support after you get her to sign the will.

From ****** to Me:**

YOU ARE FUCKING SICK, I HOPE YOU BURN IN HELL

From ME to *********:

You clearly do not have the right mind-set to enter the fast-paced industry of babysitting. I will find a babysitter that has a little bit more balls than you.

From ****** to Me:**

FUCK OFF

Engrish Tutor

Linda's original ad:

> English tutor needed for fifth grader who is struggling in English class. Must have experience in tutoring and references.

From Me to Linda:

Greeting!

Name of Me is Xiu. I very friendly and people your. Job availability, yes? Language of English, skill it as the me! For tutor, choice of the excellence one only.

Sincerity,

Xiu Yang

From Linda to Me:

What the heck are you trying to say?

From Me to Linda:

So job mine, yes? Date of starting, please.

From Linda to Me:

NO!!!

Linda missed out on a great opportunity for her child to learn a real English lesson: how to deal with people who can't speak English. It would have prepared the kid for the real world.

Livestock Model

I see ads seeking modeling jobs all the time: people who think that they are good-looking and therefore will never have to get a real job. I wanted to show them what modeling is really all about. I chose this guy because spelling errors in the ad usually mean that the writer lacks the intelligence to realize when to stop writing back to me.

Jeril's original ad:

> aspiring attractve male model looking to start career.
>
> will do any kind of modelling work for pay

From Me to Jeril:

Greetings,

I am a journalist for a popular agriculture magazine. I am currently writing an article on farming in rural America and how livestock are detrimental to the environment. I am looking to take some photographs of a person in the center of this problem. I will pay travel expenses and a small fee, but your main reward will be knowing that you are saving the environment. This would look great for any future modeling gigs you may get.

Let me know if you are available.

Thank you,

Mike

From Jeril to Me:

Hi it sounds like a intriging shoot i am very interested

i am 6'2 180 pounds

From Me to Jeril:

Jeril,

Sounds good. Are you familiar with Port Royal? Also, will you be comfortable working with livestock and the outdoors?

Mike

From Jeril to Me:

yes I am comfortable working with livestock. i live in lewistown which is very close to port royal

From Me to Jeril:

Jeril,

Excellent. I am going to need to take several pictures of you standing near cows, sheep, pigs, and horses. I also need some pictures that will illustrate the harmful effects of animals on the environment. I need a few pictures of you standing near some diseased cows, a picture of you in a pig trough, and a picture of you covered in cow manure. I have scheduled some time with a farmer to do this on Thursday afternoon. Can you meet on Thursday at 2:00?

Mike

From Jeril to Me:

Hey I am open to many things but i dont think i can do the pictures with diseased cows or the picture of me covered in cow manure. Sorry I dont think this is going to work for me.

From Me to Jeril:

Jeril,

May I ask why you can't do the pictures? I will understand if you are a vegetarian or have issues with diseased cows. I assure you all health precautions will be taken into consideration. We will have vitamin C standing by for you to eat after standing near the cow, to prevent sickness. You must understand that this is very important; I already have booked a photographer and need to get this shoot. We will pay you $300 for the shoot.

Mike

From Jeril to Me:

sorry but i cannot do it, i can do other pictures but not those ones. i must turn down your offer if the cow manure pictures are needed

From Me to Jeril:

Jeril,

I am willing to work with you. We don't need the pictures of you in the pig trough, or the pictures of you with the diseased cow. What is very important for this article and the magazine is the picture of you in cow manure. It will need to be all over your body and face, but we will make sure that it does not touch your eyes or mouth. As I am sure you are aware, cow manure is actually very organic. In some countries, cow manure is considered a delicacy. I am not asking you to eat the cow manure, but simply to cover your body in it and be photographed. It may seem dirty, but sometimes that is necessary. I've met with models who have had to do some very unconventional things to get their start in modeling. You do not want to pass on this opportunity. I am running out of time and really need you to reconsider. I am willing to offer you $500.

Mike

From Jeril to Me:

no i am not comfortable doing that. sorry

From Me to Jeril:

My final offer is $1000. How does that sound?

Mike

From Jeril to Me:

That sounds great. am I too late or no?

Success! You can put a price on a person's dignity. Everyone has their price. Everyone. Apparently the price to have a picture of you covered in cow shit published in a magazine is only $1,000.

A fun thing some old friends and I used to do was call up escort services and see how much money it would take to get the whores to do disgusting things. One time, after a long negotiation, my friend convinced a prostitute to have sex with his dog for $5,000. She even called back asking where he was, because she was at the hotel we told her to go to. I'll say it again: everyone has their price.

Snow Shoveling

Original ad:

> Im a 19 year old in desperate need of money looking for people who want their driveways shoveled. will shovel driveways for $30 and $35+ for larger ones. email me at ******** thanks!

From ME to ********:

Hi! I am in desperate need of a snow shoveler. How soon are you available?

Mike

From ******** to Me:

im ready to go any time. what do you have going on? how big is your driveway/sidewalks, stuff like that?

From ME to ********:

Actually, I don't need you for my driveway, I need you to shovel my business before 8 AM tomorrow. I own the ******** Shopping Center and need all the parking lots and sidewalks shoveled, as well as the loading area behind the stores so the trucks can make their deliveries. I don't have a shovel so you will need to bring your own, as well as salt.

From ******** to Me:

screw that! are you kidding me why dont you just hire a plow guy?

From ME to *********:

I don't have the money to hire a plow service, and I tried putting a plow on my wife's Prius but it wasn't doing a very good job. Plus, most of the plow guys I've used in the past refuse to plow for me anymore. I will pay you the full $35 for shoveling, and if it is done quickly I'll throw in a nice tip. I'll even have my wife make you some hot chocolate when you are done (with a shitload of Jameson).

From ******** to Me:

i dont care if you pay me $100 theres no fuckin way im doing that. we got like 2 feet of snow by the time id be done the snow will have melted. really how can you own a shopping center and not afford to pay a plow guy

From ME to *********:

Well, your ad said $35, so don't expect me to be paying you $100. It isn't even that hard of a job. I'll cut you a break—you won't have to shovel any of the handicapped spots. Handicapped people have no business being out in the snow anyway.

Also, I already told you, the plow guy I usually use won't plow anymore because I accidentally popped all his tires with tire spikes. I normally put spikes up after hours to prevent all those freeloading Walmart people from parking and sleeping in my parking lot, but I forgot to take them down when the plow guy came.

I'm ready to make you a final offer. If you have the entire lot shoveled by 8 AM tomorrow, I will let you park for free in that shopping center for a week. You can even park in the handicapped spots, and I assure you I won't have you towed.

From ******** to Me:

**well gee that sounds like a great deal. NOT. i dont want free parking
in that shitty shopping center its just a bunch of flower shops and
jewelry stores. if you cant get a plow guy youre shit out of luck
because nobody is going to shovel a whole damn parking lot now
leave me the fuck alone**

From ME to ********:

You teens these days have the most pathetic work ethic. You can't
pick and choose the jobs you want in the real world; you have to
take what you can get. You clearly are too lazy to be shoveling, so
why don't you go back to your house and play Xbox all day. Maybe
there is a snow shoveling video game you can play so you don't
have to go out into the scary world and actually do it.

At first I was going to leave this guy alone, but then I saw he was
charging $35 to shovel a driveway. For that price, he better repave the
driveway in gold when he is finished shoveling.

Operation: Soccer Escort

This is a pedophile or serial killer's wet dream. It was also a gold mine for me. I look for stupidity in the ads, and nothing is more stupid than a mother who is looking on the internet for a complete stranger to drive her 10-year-old daughter home every day.

Kate's original ad:

> I am in need of a reliable and SAFE driver to take my 10-year-old daughter home from after-school soccer practice starting in September and ending in late November. She needs to be taken from school in Exton to home in Bryn Mawr. It should take about an hour each day. You will be needed Mon, Tues, Thurs, and Fri. Looking for a safe driver with a clean driving record. Email at ******** with references. We can discuss compensation. Thanks!

From Me to Kate:

Good afternoon.

My name is Mike Partlow and I am very interested in this job. I have a lot of experience driving under dangerous conditions and guarantee your daughter will arrive safely at home every day.

Sincerely,

Mike Partlow

From Kate to Me:

Mr. Partlow (can I call you Mike?),

Good to know you can handle dangerous conditions . . . but there probably will not be any dangerous conditions; you are just taking my daughter down Route 3.

Tell me about yourself—are you a professional driver? Do you have any references from past jobs? What kind of car do you own? Is it reliable?

Kate

From Me to Kate:

You can call me Mike. I was never one for formalities.

A little about myself: I am 37 years old and worked as a mercenary driver in the Middle East. I escorted important clients through high-risk areas in Iraq and Afghanistan for five years. I have seen a lot of action and have ensured the safety of my clients. Out of all the jobs I have done, 90% of my clients arrived at their destination unharmed.

I have several references. I'll have one of them email you.

My car is very safe and reliable—perfect for your daughter. It is an armored 2007 Chevy Suburban. All glass has been replaced with multi-layered ballistic glass capable of stopping a 7.62 x 39 bullet dead in its tracks. The doors, roof, and floor have been reinforced with ballistic steel/composite that can withstand IED blasts and stop grenade fragmentation. This car has been put to the test and will always deliver.

Safety and protection are my #1 priority. The car is fully loaded with an HK416 assault rifle that can fire under the toughest conditions. The roof has a 40mm MK-19 automatic grenade launcher turret installed. Hopefully we won't have to use it, but it is good to have. I can't tell you how many times I've had to return fire against an enemy APC. I assure you that nobody will mess with your daughter as I escort her home from soccer practice.

Now let's discuss pay. I offer various security packages, and for your daughter I recommend my medium package, which will run you $200 an hour. I also have a minimal package that is only $125 an hour. It is entirely up to you.

Let me know,

Mike Partlow

From Kate to Me:

This has to be a joke. This isn't Baghdad, it's suburban PA.

Are you just being sarcastic? What do you really drive? I want to pay 30 bucks a day, tops.

From Me to Kate:

Kate,

Safety/protection is no joke. For $30, you are likely to get some 17-year-old kid who just got his license and will drive your daughter in his unarmored Ford Focus. I've seen a homemade bomb blow a Ford Focus into thousands of pieces, none larger than a golf ball.

My security package is well worth the $200 per trip. We will pick your daughter up in a random Suburban. Four trucks will pull up, and she will get into a random one every day. This is so the enemy does not know which one to attack. The Suburban she is in will have an armed security detail of men I have worked with in Iraq. We know what we are doing. She will be escorted in our convoy down the highway at a high rate of speed to avoid stopping in kill zones. All vehicles are equipped with an MIRT, which is used to change the traffic lights to green so we will not have to slow down. Your daughter will arrive safely in your arms no later than 20 minutes from when she is extracted from the soccer field.

Please reconsider my offer. You can't put a price on your daughter's safety.

From Kate to Me:

Stop wasting my time. Don't email me again.

(Later, from another email account under the name of Nick Walken)

From Me to Kate:

Dear Kate,

I am an old client of Mike Partlow. He told me that you wanted a reference for a job you are considering him for. Let me start off by saying that you could not have made a finer choice. Mike is the best there is. He literally saved my life countless times in Iraq. Whatever you are using him for, you have made the right choice. You will be 100% safe.

When I think about my experience with Mike, one time stands above the rest. Back in 2005, I was a contractor in Iraq and had hired Mike's security detail to escort me through Fallujah. Everything was going fine until our convoy was hit by an IED. I don't remember much, but next thing you know, I woke up in a Republican Guard prisoner camp with Mike. I thought we were goners. They took me and Mike into a hut, where at least eight armed soldiers were placing bets. They were going to make Mike and me play Russian roulette. Mike convinced a soldier to let him play with three bullets, instead of one, which I thought was crazy. Mike even put the gun to his head once and pulled the trigger. He started laughing, and the soldiers started laughing too. When they let their guard down, he immediately shot three of them in the head, grabbed one of their AKs and gunned down the other five soldiers. I didn't think we would make it out of that one alive, but thanks to Mike's heroic actions, I am here today.

You cannot go wrong with Mike Partlow. He is the best of the best. One time he killed an entire truckload of insurgents using just a fork from his salad. He makes do with what he has and will survive the worst of situations.

If you have any more questions about Mike, please don't hesitate to contact me. I owe the man my life.

Nick Walken

From Kate to Me:

what in the hell . . .

> At first, I was going to go the convicted sex offender route with Kate. That would have been too predictable, though. I decided to give her daughter undoubtedly the safest ride she could ever possibly get. It was so overwhelmingly safe that this woman probably reconsidered ever asking for child-care help again.
>
> Whenever I felt like it, I would send this woman another one of Mike Partlow's "references." Here are a few of them.

From Me to Kate:

Hello,

I am writing to you on behalf of Mike Partlow, a true American hero. I understand that you are looking to hire Mike's security services and I think that you are making an excellent choice.

I met Mike back in 2003. During our advance to Al Kut, my entire company was ambushed by rocket-propelled grenade teams and snipers coming mainly from two large buildings. We were pinned down behind an embankment. We called in for air support, but they said that they did not have any planes or choppers in the area. They said they were sending this guy Mike Partlow, and he would be there shortly. Five minutes later, he pulled up in a Suburban and walked out, calm as hell. All he said was "Where are they?" and we pointed to the buildings we spotted muzzle flash coming from. He just said "Okay" and walked over to the buildings. I don't even think he had a gun. Five minutes later, he came back and said "I took care of it" and got in his Suburban and left. Upon our assessment of the buildings, every insurgent in there was dead. Thirty-seven dead Iraqis, all with their necks snapped. I don't know how he did it.

He saved our asses that day, and I will never forget it. You should be proud to have the privilege of working with Mike. I'd recommend him to anyone.

Sincerely,

Samuel Trautman

From Me to Kate:

Dear Kate,

A good friend of mine recently contacted me saying he needed a reference for a job. I just wanted to take a few minutes to put in the good word for Mike Partlow. No matter what the job, he is your man. I first met him while I was doing some contracting work in Iraq. He was assigned to escort me to An Najaf where I was supposed to build a new school. At first, I doubted him, because he insisted on escorting me there on a motorcycle. Generally we are supposed to ride in armored cars, but Mike assured me that I would be safe. He proved this when we were attacked by over 30 Iraqi Republican Guard soldiers. Not only did he manage to kill half of them using only pepper spray, he got the rest of them to surrender and work for me while I was building the school. I don't know if it is because Mike scared them, but the Iraqi Republican Guards make great drywall installers. They did excellent work. This just goes to show you that not only is Mike Partlow a lifesaver, he is a great manager as well. He will be perfect for whatever job you are considering him for.

Thanks,

Joe

After about a month of random references glorifying Mike Partlow,
Kate finally wrote back to my original email account.

From Kate to Me:

Mike,

Please stop telling your references to email me! I already hired
someone else so tell everyone to back off. Please!

Goldfish Sitter

Jeana's original ad:

Going away on vacation? Long hours at work?
I provide professional and reliable care for your
pets. I will give your pets the TLC that they need,
so you can have peace of mind wherever you will
be. I am fully insured and care for all types of pets.
Contact me for details.

From Me to Jeana:

Hey,

I am going away for a week and need someone to take care of
my goldfish while I am gone. Do you take care of fish as well? He
doesn't need much.

Thanks,

Mike

From Jeana to Me:

**No problem, Mike. Is it just one fish, and what kind? I assume you
want me to feed the fish a few times per day, but is there anything
else you require?**

Jeana

From Me to Jeana:

Jeana,

It is just one fish, and he is a goldfish. The goldfish's name is

Genovese. He lives in a small bowl which needs to be replaced with fresh water every day. I have the water stored in a Brita filter in the fridge, but you will have to refill it when it runs out.

I have several routines I do with Genovese. Every morning at 6 AM, I take Genovese for a walk. I just walk his fishbowl around the neighborhood a few times. Make sure to cover the top of the bowl if it is raining so that his water does not get contaminated.

During the weekdays, at 10 AM, we watch Jerry Springer and the Steve Wilkos show until noon. After that, I feed him one small piece of ground beef. You need to fry the ground beef in barbecue sauce. If he doesn't eat it, it means that you overcooked it and will need to cook another piece.

After that, I put Genovese's bowl in front of my TV and put on the "Ocean Deep" episode of Planet Earth. Genovese loves watching this. It should already be in my Blu-ray player. Make sure it is played in 1080p and not 720p, because Genovese hates 720p. You will have to watch it with him and make sure you skip the part about the spider crabs, because it frightens Genovese.

Genovese doesn't need much attention until 6 PM. I usually just put on some Frank Zappa for Genovese. My CD player is right below the Blu-ray player and you will just need to switch the receiver to "CD." Make sure the volume is set exactly at 2 DB.

At 6 PM, you will need to feed Genovese again. For dinner, I usually make a portobello steak and give Genovese a tiny piece. There should be some in my freezer, but if I am out, you will have to go to Acme to get more.

After this, I put Genovese on the dresser next to my bed. You will need to sleep next to him so he feels comfortable, but please try not to mess up my bed.

On Sunday night, you will have to watch "The Sopranos" with Genovese. I am aware that it is not on TV anymore, but Genovese was so upset when we stopped watching it that I had to buy all six seasons on DVD. Right now, we are on the third episode of season four. It is very necessary that you put this on at exactly 9 on Sunday night; otherwise Genovese will jump out of the bowl and start flopping around.

Please let me know if you have any other questions. I am going away next Wednesday for a week, so will you be available then? Also, what are your rates?

Thanks,

Mike

From Jeana to Me:

Do you really do all that every day? That's very excessive for a fish.

From Me to Jeana:

Jeana,

Yes, I do that every day. I love my goldfish and want him to live a happy life. Is this going to be a problem?

Mike

From Jeana to Me:

Honestly, yes, it will be a problem. I can't dedicate my entire day to taking care of one fish.

From Me to Jeana:

Jeana,

Now I see that by "professional and reliable," you really mean "bitchy and lazy." Thanks for nothing.

Mike

From Jeana to Me:

So you think I'm lazy because I won't watch TV with your fish and cook it steak? Sorry, I'm not eccentric enough to do all that stupid

stuff for your fish! I got news for you—fish can't hear and they don't have long-term memory. That means your fish doesn't give a crap about frank zappa or the sopranos! For crying out loud, it is just a freaking fish!

From Me to Jeana:

Jeana,

I sure as hell hope that you don't have any children. If you raise your kids with that mind-set, they are probably going to turn out just as lazy as you are.

I guess I am just going to have to cancel my vacation.

Mike

> For someone who promised to give my pets nothing but tender love and care, she sure was a rude bitch.

Kons for Kids

I love finding ads where the victim is looking for someone to care for their children. This woman thinks that just because she asks for references, it will make sure that her kids are in good hands. Anyone can make up a reference. Whatever happened to asking a neighbor's teenage daughter to babysit?

original ad:

> ## CHILDCARE NEEDED
>
> looking for a responsible and dedicated person to babysit my two children during the week. you will be needed monday through friday, from 7 AM to 4:30 PM. email me at ******** and we can talk about pay. DO NOT EMAIL ME UNLESS YOU HAVE REFERENCES.

From Me to ********:

Hi there! Are you still looking for someone to fill your babysitter position?

Mike

From ******** to Me:

yes i am. please send your info and any past expereince you have.

From Me to ********:

Actually, I am not the one applying for the position. I run a reha-bilitation program for good people who are trying to enter society again, and I have a few candidates who I think would be able to watch your kids. They will work for a much cheaper rate than a professional babysitter, but will still deliver professional service.

Mike

From ******** to Me:

what kind of rehab program do you run? injured people or something like that? if you are talking about drug addicts than forget it.

From Me to ********:

Absolutely not! Don't worry, I would never even dare consider having drug addicts watch your children. They are children, for pete's sake!

My rehabilitation program is called Kons for Kids. We help get ex-convicts back on the right track again by giving them second chances that they deserve. We help them experience the joy of working with children and helping the community. It is often difficult for these ex-cons to get jobs after being released from a correctional facility, but it is a requirement while they are on parole.

We have seen lots of success with the program. Most of our clients are extremely satisfied with their ex-con. Despite the negative image that the public has of ex-cons, they really are loving, caring people.

I have two potential clients in your area, if you are interested. Here is a little info about them:

Derek Schillinger—Derek is a 43-year-old male from the Delaware County area. Just released after serving 17 of 25 years for two counts of third-degree murder. Derek loves to laugh, read, and take long walks on the beach.

Timothy Beecher—Tim is a 36-year-old male who was just released after serving 12 years of his 15-year sentence for armed robbery and assault with a deadly weapon. Tim was released on good behavior and is ready to get back into the real world. Tim enjoys working with kids; he has six kids of his own with various women in the tristate area. Before his conviction, Tim was a midlevel cocaine dealer. He knows a lot about economics and business and would be able to give your children a great education while watching them.

I look forward to working with you. Please let me know which person you are interested in, and I will give his parole officer a call.

Thanks!

Mike

From ****** to Me:**

wow. kons for kids? that is the stupidest thing ive ever heard!!! who the fuck would let a murderer watch their kids!

From Me to ******:**

KFK is a very respectable program. I'm guessing from your apparent issues with murderers that you aren't interested in Derek. Before you completely rule him out, I would like to point out that he was convicted of third-degree murder, which is the most harmless kind of murder. Third-degree murder isn't premeditated murder; it's usually just accidental murder. I talked to Derek, and he said he didn't mean to kill the guy; he just wanted to hurt him. Please give him another chance.

If you don't want him watching your kids, though, I'll understand. Should I tell Tim you are interested instead?

Mike

From ****** to Me:**

i dont want tim or derek or any of the other lunatics you try to pass off as babysitters! murder is murder it doesnt matter which way you put it now leave me the fuck alone!

From Me to *********:

I already told Tim that he got the job. Please don't make me have to give him the bad news.

From Me to *********:

Are you still there? It has been three days, and Tim wants to know when he can start working again.

From Me to *********:

Well, I hope you are happy. I had to tell Tim that you weren't willing to give him a second chance. Tim got so angry that he tried to stab me with a fountain pen. Needless to say, that was considered a violation of his parole and he has been sent back to his correctional facility to serve the remainder of his sentence. You essentially ruined Tim's life, after he was ready to get back on the right track. You are a horrible person.

Mike

> Kons for Kids really showed promise as a great rehabilitation program. Unfortunately, due to responses like this woman's selfishness, the program had to be shut down.

Looking for a Ride

IT AMUSES ME TO SEE just how much shit people are willing to put up with in order to get a cheap ride across the country. I usually start out by writing to my victims sounding completely normal. It might seem a bit odd that I insist on listening to cassette tapes I've recorded of me and my girlfriend having sex or that I can only drive with the heat on full blast even though it is the middle of the summer.

Some people are willing to put aside these things, knowing that they will be getting a ride from, say, Philly to Atlanta for $50. Then they find out that we'll have to avoid Maryland, because I have warrants. Warrants for what? Who knows? I'll leave that up to the victims' imagination; they usually assume the worst. Or perhaps I will be on horse tranquilizers while I am driving. Maybe I want to stop every two hours to have sex with a prostitute at a truck stop.

Now, the victims start to get a bit worried. They start to wonder: is it really worth saving a few bucks to be riding with a horny, drugged-up criminal? How bad do they need the ride? Are they even saving that much money when I tell them that they will be splitting the gas costs for my Hummer that gets six miles to the gallon? Is it really necessary to make a "quick stop" in Detroit when traveling from Boston to Baltimore? At this point, the victims usually realize that they are better off taking a train or flying. That, or they simply tell me to fuck myself.

Ride to Bonnaroo

Kathy's original ad:

> i need a ride from philly to bonnaroo in manchester, TN!
> i will throw up some cash for gas. i dont have that much stuff
> either. i am a down ass chick and will be fun to ride with!

From Me to Kathy:

Hey! I'm taking my truck down to Bonnaroo and should have an extra seat. I'm planning on leaving Wednesday afternoon. Does this work for you?

From Kathy to Me:

yes that is fine! thank you! where do you live? i can meet you somewhere if it is easier for you.

From Me to Kathy:

I live in West Philadelphia, born and raised. I can meet you anywhere you want. So far it is me, you, my friend Josh, and his friends Steve and Rob. It should be a fun ride!

From Kathy to Me:

great! how big is your truck? i may have a lot of stuff.

From Me to Kathy:

My truck is pretty big. It is a Mazda Miata and it can hold around 3 people. You will probably have to sit on Steve's lap. He's fat though, so it will be somewhat comfortable to sit on. Are you attractive? My only concern is that Steve may get turned on when you are sitting on his lap. If this is an issue, you can sit on Josh's lap because he is gay. The only problem with that is that if you are fat, you may crush him because he is a small dude. But if you are fat you can probably just sit on Steve's lap without him getting aroused.

From Kathy to Me:

what?! how the hell are you going to fit 5 people in a miata? that isnt a truck! i dont want to sit on anyones lap.

From Me to Kathy:

Oh, I get it. You are one of those Ford fanboys that likes to hate on Miatas. That's okay, I'm not too adamant about Mazdas. If you don't want to sit on Steve or Josh's lap, you can sit on mine, since I have a girlfriend and won't try anything. You will have to drive since my legs will be stuck, though. That's probably better, anyway, since my license is revoked until 2012, and I have a few warrants. Do you know how to drive stick? If you don't, I can teach you. You can pick it up in like five minutes.

From Kathy to Me:

no im not driving are you fucking kidding me? this sounds like a horrible ride. ill find another ride thanks but no thanks. i still dont get how you are going to cram 4 dudes into a miata.

From Me to Kathy:

Do you have a car? You can just follow us down there in your car if you want more room. I take the long way, however, since if I get pulled over in Kentucky or Virginia I will probably go to jail. We are going around, through Missouri. Missouri is really nice though!

From Kathy to Me:

IF I HAD A CAR I WOULDNT NEED A FUCKING RIDE
THIS IS RIDICULOUS IM DONE TALKING TO YOU

I am glad Kathy didn't ride with us; she was very ungrateful.
I offered to drive her over 800 miles for free, yet she complained
about the most insignificant shit.

Drunken Rideshare

> I need a ride from Baltimore to New Orleans next weekend. I will be bringing just two bags. You will be compensated.

From Me to Steven:

Hey!

If you still need a ride, I am headed to New Orleans next Friday and am looking for some company on the way down. I want to leave at 9 AM, and we will split the cost of gas and tolls.

Mike

From Steven to Me:

Hi,

I do still need a ride. Sounds good to me. Would you be able to pick me up at my apartment, or do you prefer to meet me somewhere?

Steven

From Me to Steven:

Steve,

I can do either, whatever works for you. I am going to stop and pick up a few cases of beer for the ride down and maybe a bottle of whiskey or something. If you want, I can get you some booze too. What do you drink?

Mike

From Steven to Me:

I don't drink . . . You're not gonna be drinking while driving, are you?

From Me to Steven:

Steve,

Of course I am. Don't worry though; I am an exceptional drunk driver.

If you don't want to drink, that's fine. That actually works out better, because the court ordered me to get this goddamn ignition interlock thing installed on my car, which means I have to get a sober person to blow into it to start my car. I usually just pay some random person walking down the street five bucks to do it, but you can take care of that.

You sure you don't just want a twelve-pack of something? It is going to be a long ride.

Mike

From Steven to Me:

Are you kidding? If you are going to be drunk, then forget it. That is a terrible idea.

From Me to Steven:

Awwww c'mon, Steve, don't be such a little bitch about this. I shouldn't have said anything. Don't worry, I usually only have about 7 or 8 beers an hour. I'll be fine. I just wanted to make the ride a little more fun, because frankly, you sound boring. The fact that you go by "Steven" instead of "Steve" makes you come off as boring and a little bit of a prick. You not wanting to drink just confirmed this.

So where do you live? I can swing by and pick you up around 8:30 on Friday.

From Steven to Me:

I'm not interested anymore—you're a scumbag! You should be the one looking for a ride . . .

From Me to Steven:

Well, at least I have a car. Do you have a car, Steve? Would you like to give me a ride in your boring sober-mobile? We can drink cranberry juice, listen to AM radio, and talk about golf.

From Steven to Me:

You shouldn't have a damn car! How you have yet to crash it is anyone's guess! Stop bothering me with this, it isn't going to happen!

Despite Steven's decision not to ride with me, I still got hammered and made it to New Orleans. I didn't exactly remember driving there, but I'm sure it was a safe trip.

Hummer Rideshare

Chris's original ad:

> looking for a ride from wilmington to manhattan next
> wednesday, any time during the day is good. I will pay
> for all your gas as compensation.

From Me to Chris:

Hello,

I am driving to NYC for a business meeting around 10 AM on
Wednesday and would be able to give you a ride. Let me know if
you still need one.

Mike

From Chris to Me:

mike, that sounds great. where do you want to meet to pick me up?
i can meet you anywhere in wilmington. also, how much do you
want for gas?

chris

From Me to Chris:

Chris,

I shouldn't need too much money for gas. I drive a Hummer H2
with a swapped motor, so gas really isn't a problem. It gets about
4 mpg highway and only takes premium, so I'd say about $100
should cover it.

Mike

From Chris to Me:

what do you mean gas isn't a problem? 4 mpg is ridiculous. I was expecting to pay like 20 or 30 bucks tops! sorry but I'll have to pass.

From Me to Chris:

If you only want to pay 30 bucks, that can get you as far as Exit 7 on the Jersey Turnpike. I can drop you off there, and you can hitchhike the rest of the way. I'm pretty sure hitchhiking is still legal in NJ so it shouldn't be a problem for you. I can pick you up on Naaman's Road in Wilmington by the Target shopping center around 9:30.

From Chris to Me:

are you serious? no I don't want to be dropped off in the middle of the turnpike. forget it.

From Me to Chris:

Okay, I can give you a ride to Manhattan for $30, but in return, we need to stop at this guy's house in New Brunswick to get some money that he owes me. He's been dodging my calls, so he probably won't be too willing to give the money when we show up at his house. I need you to stand there and look intimidating so he realizes we mean business. How big are you? You should be at least 5'11 and 200 lbs. You can bring a big friend if you are scrawny, but you should ask him to throw up some gas money too.

From Chris to Me:

what the fuck is wrong with you? you sound like a drug dealer. i don't want to ride to manhattan with you.

From Me to Chris:

Chris, I'm sorry that you have turned down my ride. I think you should change your ad to avoid any further confusion. I rewrote it for you so all you have to do is click "edit" and then paste this where the original ad is:

"scrawny man, not capable of intimidating people, looking for a ride from wilmington to new york. not willing to be reasonable in compensation for gas. will most likely complain about stupid stuff the whole ride up."

From Chris to Me:

fuck off, *asshole*

I bet Chris will think twice the next time he volunteers to pay for all the gas. Here is a tip: if you are ever driving someone and they tell you they will pay for gas, it is basically the green light for you to drive like a complete asshole. Do burnouts, rev your engine at red lights, and speed up to 90 mph, slow back down to 40, and then back to 90 over and over again. What would normally take half a tank of gas ends up costing the poor volunteer over three times that amount.

Fat Bitch Won't Ride the Bus

Melanie's original ad:

> im looking for ride from the philadelphia area to pittsburgh next friday. i will split the cost of gas with you. I am female and would prefer to ride with another female or young (21-ish) person.

From Me to Melanie:

Hey! I am going to Pittsburgh and can give you a ride. Can you meet me at 30th St. Station 11 AM on Friday? By the way, I'm 21, so you don't have to worry about riding with some old creeper.

Mike

From Melanie to Me:

hey mike! that sounds good. how much do you want for gas? let me get your number so we can work out the details.

From Me to Melanie:

Melanie,

I was thinking around $70 should cover it. Unfortunately I do not have a cell phone because I accidentally forgot to take my pants off when I was taking a bath last night and forgot my cell phone was in the pocket. It won't turn on! Could you just stand outside of the west entrance with a sign that says "I'm Melanie"? I'll look for you.

Mike

From Melanie to Me:

wow, i wasnt expecting to pay $70! why so much? i was thinking more around 30-35 bucks! also im not standing out there with a sign lol.

From Me to Melanie:

Melanie, I'm sorry but the price is not negotiable. Unfortunately the cheapest bus ticket is $70. Do you want to just meet me on the bus if you don't want to stand out there with a sign?

From Melanie to Me:

what?! i didnt want to ride a bus! i thought you were driving a car to pittsburgh. wtf dude

From Me to Melanie:

Well, shit, Melanie, I didn't think you would be so picky about what kind of vehicle you wanted to ride in. If price is an issue, I can sneak you on the bus. I've done it before with my son. I have a duffel bag that is pretty big, and you can just hide inside it and not move and they will load you under the bus. I'll make sure that they put you on top of all the other luggage so you aren't crushed. You can have my video iPod to stay entertained during the bus ride. It has the first season of "Deadwood" on it. You aren't fat, are you? I don't want the bag to rip from underneath when they lift it up.

Mike

From Melanie to Me:

are you fucking with me? this has to be a joke. there is no fucking way im doing that.

From Me to Melanie:

Oh, you aren't a "Deadwood" fan? I think I have the Ben Affleck hit "Gigli" on my iPod if you wanted to watch that instead.

From Melanie to Me:

NO! IM NOT SNEAKING ON TO THE FUCKING BUS IN A GODDAMN SUITCASE

From Me to Melanie:

Okay, I didn't realize you were so sensitive about your weight. If you can't fit in the duffel bag, that's fine. I just went and ordered you the bus ticket. It is pretty much first-come first-serve for seating on the bus. You can sit next to me if you want, but I want the window seat. I also have to get up a lot to pee so you will have to get up so I can squeeze out.

From Melanie to Me:

IM NOT RIDING THE BUS! I'LL FIND ANOTHER RIDE

From Me to Melanie:

Well, you owe me $70 for the ticket! I can't return it!

From Melanie to Me:

I NEVER SAID TO BUY IT! THAT IS YOUR FAULT, DUDE. GOODBYE

If Melanie was smart, she would have stopped responding as soon as I told her that I forgot to take my pants off while I took a bath. Thankfully, she was an idiot. This email exchange lasted until the night before she wanted to go to Pittsburgh. It would have been ironic if she wasted so much time arguing with me that she couldn't find a ride and had to take the bus anyway.

Luring Victims

SOMETIMES I PUT MY OWN AD
up and let the victims come to me. I set the bait
and they fall for it hook, line, and sinker. Posting
the ad myself catches the victims entirely off
guard. When people put their own ad up, they prob-
ably get a ton of shitty offers. By the time I get to them, they are
already pissed off and defensive, ready to snap at the slightest
thing. If someone is trying to sell their Cadillac, an asshole like
me who wants to rent the car and use it to get laid is probably
the last thing they feel like dealing with. However, when I put the
ad up, the people are not yet tired of dealing with assholes on the
internet. I get fresh victims who are really hoping to buy what I am
selling. Even once I start fucking with them, some don't understand that they should just stop replying. They get confused. Why
is this guy being an asshole? Doesn't he want to sell his car? He
must just not realize he's being a dick.

Having all the victims come to me gives me power to decide
which ones I think are stupid enough to fuck with. The guy who
says "I am interest to buy car" most likely is an idiot and will fall
for my shit. Putting up my own ad just makes everything so much
easier for me.

Bad Photographer

I put up a purposefully vague ad so that I would get more victims emailing me with questions about the car.

My original ad:

> 2000 Acura RL for sale. $3000.

From ****** to Me:**

hey do you have any pics of the car? and what is the mileage?

From Me to ******:**

Hey,

Give me a few minutes and I will go out and take pictures of the car and the odometer for you.

Thanks,

Mike

From Me to ******:**

Okay, I've taken a few pictures of the car. I have attached them in this email. Would you like to stop by and take a look at the car?

Mike

Attachments:

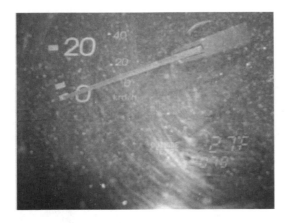

From ******** to Me:

can you take better pictures? i cant tell anything from those.

From Me to ********:

Well, aren't you picky. Sorry I'm not a professional photographer. Those are the best pictures you are going to get. What is your problem with them?

From ******** to Me:

are you retarded? your finger is blocking the entire freaking car in two of the pictures! i dunno what you did to screw up the picture of the odometer but come on, man, it cant be that hard to work a freaking camera.

From Me to ********:

Fine, I'll go outside and take another picture. But this is the last one I am going to take because it is freezing cold out there and very windy.

From Me to ********:

Here is a better picture. I hope my finger didn't get in the way for this one.

Attachment :

From ******** **to Me:**

fuck you too you fucking piece of shit

I usually don't lose my temper on anyone, but this guy really offended me when he insulted my ability to take pictures. I consider myself a good photographer and take pride in my work.

Annoying Car

My intentionally unclear ad lured in another victim . . .

My original ad:

2000 Acura RL for sale. $3000.

From Dave to Me:

I'm interested in the Acura. Can you tell me about it?

From Me to Dave:

Hi Dave. What would you like to know about the car?

Mike

From Dave to Me:

I would like to know:

- color (interior/exterior)
- mileage
- condition
- damage (interior/exterior)
- options
- why you are selling it

Thank you.

From Me to Dave:

Dave,

The Acura is silver, it has 150,000 miles, is in good condition, there are a few scratches (I had to commute to New Jersey, and people drive like morons there). It comes with power everything, 6-disc CD changer in the console, heated leather seats, and cup holders.

I am selling it for several reasons. For one, I spilled coffee on the stereo while I was getting road head, and it messed up the electronics in the stereo. I'm not sure exactly why this happens, but now the car plays my CD on repeat at full volume no matter what I do. As soon as the car turns on, it blasts music at an unbearable volume (the Bose sound system can get very loud) over and over again. The CD happens to be a single of "What Is Love." It can get annoying, but it is great if you are a Haddaway fan.

I am also selling it because the airbag will randomly deploy while I am driving. It really hurts sometimes. One time it even broke my nose. The mechanic said the coffee spill altered a lot of the electronics in the car and makes it do weird things. I don't have the money to keep replacing the airbag, nor do I have the money to fix the CD player problem. So if you can deal with "What Is Love" playing at full volume and randomly taking an airbag to the face, then this is the perfect car for you.

Let me know when you want to come check it out.

Mike

From Dave to Me:

That is um . . . very strange. Do you know how much it would cost to fix those things?

From Me to Dave:

The mechanic I took it to refused to work on it because he "hates that fucking song." I think if you wrap enough duct tape around the steering wheel, it should prevent the airbag from deploying again. If you want, I can duct tape the steering wheel for you and throw in a pair of heavy-duty earmuffs to block out the noise. The earmuffs work great—I usually wear them while I'm mowing the lawn or if my wife is yelling at me, and I can't hear a thing. I'll give you the duct tape and the earmuffs for an extra $50.

Mike

From Dave to Me:

I don't want to wear earmuffs while I drive. I'm going to have to pass on this, thanks anyway.

I just wanted to see if someone would drive a car that blasts annoying music and pummels the driver in the face with an airbag. Now I have my answer.

Wrong Number

My ad lured in quite possibly the stupidest victim yet. Sensing stupidity from his first response, I thought it would be fun to see how many different Pizza Huts I could convince him to call.

My original ad:

> 2000 Acura RL for sale. $3000.

From Muhammad to Me:

I AM INTEREST TO BUY CAR DO YOU HAVE PHONE.

THANKS

From Me to Muhammad:

Yes. My phone number is ***-***-1130. You can call me anytime.

Mike

From Muhammad to Me:

I THINK YOU GAVE ME MISTAKE PHONE.

From Me to Muhammad:

Whoops, my mistake. That was my old number, which for some reason was still in my email's auto-complete. My new number is ***-***-8442.

Mike

From Muhammad to Me:

MISTAKE PHONE AGAIN. DO YOU KNOW YOUR PHONE.

From Me to Muhammad:

I am terribly sorry. I forgot that my number changed again after I moved here. I haven't learned the new number yet, so I keep forgetting it. My new number is ***-***-8859.

From Muhammad to Me:

I CALL EVERY TIME IT IS FOR PIZZA. YOUR PHONE MISTAKE? NOT WRONG PHONE THANKS.

From Me to Muhammad:

My mistake again. I actually read the number above mine in the phone book, which was the number for Pizza Hut. I'm sorry. I found my real number now, I tried calling it and it works. It is ***-***-2861.

From Me to Muhammad:

I have not heard from you. Are you still interested in buying the car? Please let me know.

From Muhammad to Me:

NO EVERY TIME I CALL IT IS PIZZA. PIZZA ALL THE TIME. YOU AREN'T PHONE NUMBER

He's got a good point there; I am not phone number.
The last phone number I gave him was actually my real number.
I just had to hear what this jackass sounded like. When he called me,
I answered pretending to be Pizza Hut. I heard some angry Arabic
shouting and then he hung up.

Now that I have his number, I am going to occasionally call him and
ask him where he wants his pizza delivered.

Sentimental Seat

My original ad:

> 2000 Acura RL for sale. $3000.

From Damian to Me:

hi,

i am looking for a car right now, can you send details about your car?

damian

From Me to Damian:

Hi Damian,

The car is a silver Acura 3.5 RL in excellent condition. It has 150,000 highway miles on it, just passed inspection, and has brand-new tires, heated leather seats, and a 6-disc CD changer.

Thanks,

Mike

From Damian to Me:

will you take $2500 for it in cash?

From Me to Damian:

Damian,

I will take $2500 for it, but I would like to keep the front driver seat. It is a very sentimental seat for me, as it is where I lost my virginity. I will unbolt the seat before you buy the car.

Mike

From Damian to Me:

what? no, i want the seat. dont take the seat out. i cant drive it
without the seat

From Me to Damian:

I must have that seat. You can go get another seat for the car
somewhere else, but I am keeping this one. I can give you a folding
chair or some pillows to put where the seat used to be. It should
be just as comfortable, if not even more comfortable.

From Damian to Me:

that is stupid what are you gonna do with the seat once its out of
the car hang it on your wall? who cares if you had sex in it some
things you just gotta let go man what are you like some loser that
never gets laid

From Me to Damian:

Damian,

I resent that accusation. I get laid at least once every two weeks.
I don't know how important you consider sex, but for me, losing
my virginity was a very defining moment in my life. It is a very
sacred and meaningful moment to me, and I must have the seat
to remind me of it. I remember back when it happened in 2001. I
had just bought the Acura and got some cash back from the dealership. I took the car and the extra cash down to Atlantic City and
pulled up to the first prostitute I saw. Her name was Rhonda. We
made sweet love on that seat for exactly half an hour and it was
life-changing for me. That is why I must have this seat, and I won't
sell the car to you any other way.

From Damian to Me:

you sure are a classy guy you know what keep the car and the seat
and good luck selling it without the drivers seat loser

Caught!

My original ad:

2000 Acura RL for sale. $3000.

From Daniel to Me:

Hi is your car still for sale

From Me to Daniel:

Yes it is. Would you like to come by and check it out?

From Daniel to Me:

oh fuck that I remember you mother fucker, what the fuck is your deal? are you a car salesman that is trying to get fired?

From Me to Daniel:

I believe you have me mistaken for someone else. I am an honest man that is just trying to sell an old car.

From Daniel to Me:

yeah bulshit. i wanted to buy your camry and you told me that i would have to come to your dealership and fight all the other inter-ested buyers in a boxing match. dont you think I dont remember your email address, asshole.

This was bound to happen eventually. This is why you should always change email addresses when fucking with people.

Items Wanted
and For Sale

THIS SECTION OF THE ONLINE classifeds is for people who want to sell their useless shit, as well as people who are looking for shit to buy. My goal is to make their transaction a very difficult and absurd experience for them. Most of these ad posters are seemingly innocent until I find a way to irritate them, and then their true colors show. Some people get outright offended, while others deem it necessary to tell me off and call me hurtful names.

Most people who put up wanted ads are looking for a bargain on basic things like a refrigerator or a car. However, some people want something that is a little bit more specific, like guard dogs, organic meat, or vintage liquor bottles—stuff that not a lot of people are selling. They probably aren't getting many responses, so they are more likely to at least respond to me, even if it is just to tell me to go fuck myself.

Coffee Maker Fight

Original ad:

> mr. coffee coffee maker for sale. includes digital
> display with clock and timer. $25

From Me to ********:

Hello,

I would like to purchase your coffee machine. I will pay the $25 in cash. When are you free to meet?

Thanks,

Mike

From ******** to Me:

sorry mike i aldedy sold it to someone else they are picking it up tonite

From Me to ********:

When are they picking it up? I can be there an hour earlier with cash.

Mike

From ******** to Me:

no sorry i alredy told them they could have it

From Me to ********:

Tell the other buyer that I am challenging him to a fight. You let us fight in your front yard, and the winner of the fight will get to buy the coffee maker. Make sure you tell the other guy not to bring any weapons or brass knuckles or anything like that.

Mike

From ****** to Me:**

so you want to fight a grown man for a $25 coffee maker what is wrong with you? just look for another ad i saw alot for other coffee makers jeez

From Me to ******:**

That is not an option. You tell the other guy that I have challenged him to a fight. If he is more of a man than you are, he should accept and we will settle this dispute like gentlemen over a good old-fashioned match of fisticuffs.

Mike

From ****** to Me:**

im a woman you retard and im not having a boxing fight in my house over a damn coffee maker

From Me to ******:**

Oh, that explains everything. Put your husband or boyfriend on; I want to talk to him instead. You just don't understand anything about how online classified transactions work. It is perfectly normal to fight someone else for rights to an item for sale. One time I had to beat the hell out of an old lady to get a $10 tennis racket for my son, but we settled it like adults and I won fair and square. I even had to duel a gentleman once. He was too slow to the draw, so now I am the proud owner of the pull-out sofa that I keep in my den. This is simply the proper way to do sales when you have two competing buyers.

Mike

From ****** to Me:**

read carefuly you psycho meatheaded jerk off YOUR NOT GETTING
THE COFFEE MAKER

This woman obviously wanted a fight since she left the ad online even
though she had already sold the item. She must have realized that I
am an experienced fighter and gotten scared.

High-Rise Fridge Delivery

Marty's original ad:

> I bought this GE refrigerator a few years ago, but just
> got a new one for my kitchen and no longer need it. It
> still works perfectly and is very large, perfect as your
> main fridge for a kitchen. I'm asking $300 for it. I am
> located in Brooklyn, but will be willing to deliver it up
> to 25 miles for a small fee.

From Me to Marty:

Hello,

I am very interested in your fridge. Is it still available? If so, how much would you charge to deliver it to my place in the city?

Mike

From Marty to Me:

Yes, Mike, it is still available. I will deliver it for an extra $50. Where is your place located?

From Me to Marty:

I want it delivered to my office on the 67th floor of the Chrysler Building. Now I am pretty sure that the fridge won't fit in the elevator, and if it does, it would exceed the weight capacity, so you will have to carry it up the stairs. I hope this won't be a problem.

When can you deliver it? I work Monday–Friday 9–5 and can be there any time. I do need it sooner rather than later, however.

From Marty to Me:

That is absurd. I'm not going to heave this very heavy fridge up 67 flights of stairs. Doesn't your building have a cargo/utility elevator?

From Me to Marty:

Marty, you don't have to lug it up 67 flights of stairs. There is a loading bay around back that starts on the 2nd floor, and I'm pretty sure this building does not count the 13th floor. So you are really only carrying it up 65 flights of stairs. There is a cargo elevator, but building management has told me that I am never allowed to use it again after I attempted to bring my motorcycle up to my office. They don't let just anyone use it anymore, so that isn't an option.

From Marty to Me:

Absolutely not. Do you have any idea how heavy this thing is? Why do you even need a full-size fridge in your office? Just buy one of those small mini-fridges.

From Me to Marty:

Marty,

You are obviously not a very good salesman if you are suggesting I buy something else instead of your product. How is that working out for you? Do you make a lot of money that way?

Not that it is any of your business, but I cannot afford rent in my apartment anymore and am slowly trying to move into my office so I can live out of there. I plan on disguising the fridge as a filing cabinet so my company will not get suspicious. If anyone asks you what you are doing when you are moving it into my office, just tell them that you are delivering my new filing cabinet. Try to tuck the power cord under the fridge so they don't realize that it is actually a fridge.

How does next Tuesday work? I am free all day.

Mike

From Marty to Me:

Mike, I don't think you understood me. I am NOT delivering the fridge to your office. It's way too big and heavy, and I doubt you will find anyone willing to carry it up to the 67th floor.

From Me to Marty:

Marty,

I'm sorry, I must have misread your ad. I could have sworn it said "will be willing to deliver it up to 25 miles for a small fee." Am I crazy, or did your ad say that?

I don't recall it saying "will be willing to deliver it as long as your building isn't too big and scary for my weak little body to carry it."

From Marty to Me:

Hey listen, asshole. You are a fucking idiot if you honestly think somebody will do this. It has nothing to do with strength—it is just an insane request. The only way you will get a fucking fridge up there is with an elevator. Fuck off.

From Me to Marty:

Marty, I get what you are saying. It doesn't have anything to do with strength, because even my 120-pound ex-wife could carry this thing up. It is clearly a lack of motivation. You need to be in the right mind-set to be able to do this.

Tell you what, I'll stand behind you as you carry it up and shout encouraging motivational words at you to keep you going. I'll say things like "C'mon, Marty, you can do it! You're almost there!" and "Don't give up!" I'll even bring a few bottles of Gatorade in case you get thirsty. What flavor do you want? I have frost and orange, but I really don't recommend orange because it doesn't even taste like Gatorade.

So see you Tuesday?

Mike

From Marty to Me:

Shut the fuck up.

Soon after this conversation, Marty changed his ad to include "WILL NOT CARRY IT UP STAIRS SO DON'T EVEN ASK!" I would have given him a nice tip if he actually did carry it up to the 67th floor of the Chrysler Building. He'd probably have to carry it right back down, though, because I don't actually work there.

Loving Boyfriend

> Cubic zirconia ring, princess cut,
> 14k white gold band, asking $100 or best offer.

From Me to Trisha:

Hello,

I am interested in your cubic zirconia ring but I wanted to get your opinion first. Do you think that I can convince a woman that this ring is a diamond?

Thanks,

Mike

From Trisha to Me:

If she knows anything about jewelry, then no. If she took it to a jewelry store, they would tell her it is a fake. How important is this woman to you?

From Me to Trisha:

She's my girlfriend, but for the last five years, she has been going on and on about marriage, so I figured I'd propose to her to shut her up. The thing is, I looked at engagement rings and they are really expensive. This ring looks good to me, but I want to be sure that she thinks I spent a lot of money on it. She said she always wanted a big diamond, but I don't feel like paying for that shit. Would you be able to fake a jewelry store receipt that says I spent a reasonable amount of money on it?

From Trisha to Me:

Wow, you sound like a real jerk! You are supposed to spend three months' salary on an engagement ring and you've had FIVE YEARS to do it! An engagement ring is supposed to be a symbol of your love for your woman. It is something she will wear for the rest of her life. Do you really want it to be a cheap $100 ring?

From Me to Trisha:

Three months' salary? That's like $60,000! Fuck, I'd rather spend that money on an endless supply of prostitutes! You women are insane when it comes to a stupid piece of jewelry. I guess you aren't going to fake a receipt for me. I'll take the ring, but I better be able to take the CZ stone off it and put it on another ring band so I can sell this white gold band for some money.

And by the way, your math sucks. I've been dating her for five years. Are you suggesting that I should have proposed to her on our first date? You seem like one of those crazy psycho chicks that thinks about marriage on the first date, so I wouldn't put it past you.

From Trisha to Me:

How can you be so cheap when you make $20k a month! I refuse to sell you the ring. Get her a real ring—she deserves better!

From Trisha to Me:

P.S. Fuck you!

From Me to Trisha:

You bitch. Don't tell me what to do with my money. FYI I need that money to pay for my gambling addiction and to pay off payments for my endangered snow leopard carpet that I furnished my house with. Thanks for wasting my time, you were a real help.

I'm impressed that Trisha actually got so angry that she refused to sell me the ring. I think the endangered snow leopard carpet made her too furious to even respond further. It is probably for the best that I didn't mention the giant panda fur lining in my shotgun case or my ceiling fans made out of blue whale fins. Yes, they do exist, and the breeze feels that much cooler when I know it came from an endangered animal.

Turtle Sandbox

> looking for someone to assemble a wooden swing
> set I have recently purchased. you must bring your
> own tools

From Me to John:

Hey,

I saw you are looking for someone to assemble your wooden swing set. First off, I must say that a swing set is a horrible toy for a child. I had a swing set as a kid and broke three of my ribs and tore my knee ligament on it. My career in Little League soccer was ruined. I recommend that you get your child a sandbox. I have an old sandbox that I am not using and would be willing to sell to you for $300. It is an awesome sandbox. It is shaped like a turtle, and the lid is part of the turtle too. It comes filled with beautiful sand from a beach on Coney Island, NY. Let me know if you are interested.

Tim

From John to Me:

i dont want your sandbox. i already bought the swing set for my kid and am sticking with that. its your own damn fault you got hurt on your swing set.

From Me to John:

Actually it is not my fault. The swing set had a faulty design and the swing came off while I was in the air, and I was sent flying into oncoming traffic. I am lucky to be alive. If you do not want your son mangled by a Dodge Caravan, then you should buy my sandbox instead. Sandboxes are 100% safe.

Tim

From John to Me:

fuck your sandbox. i want my kid to have fun, not to sit in some dirty ass sand from new york. i am not an idiot and will not set up my swing set where my child can be thrown into oncoming traffic.

From Me to John:

Well, it sounds like you won't set up your swing set at all without my help. Are you a quadriplegic? Why are you incapable of putting a swing set together?

If you are a quadriplegic and I have offended you, I am sorry. In that case, would you be interested in my sandbox for your crippled body to relax in? Seeing as you can't use the swing set anyway, it would be way more practical for you.

From John to Me:

FUCK OFF STOP EmailING ME

I was simply trying to do the right thing here—trying to prevent a child from getting seriously injured. Swing sets are wooden death traps in disguise. It is a shame that this father ignored my warnings in blatant disregard for his son's safety.

Deadly Guard Dog

Kevin's original ad:

> looking for a guard dog that can protect my business
> (possibly a german shepherd or a doberman). the dog
> must be brave and able to be trained to bark or attack
> unwanted intruders. i take great care of all my pets and
> promise the dog will be in good hands. thanks!

From Me to Kevin:

Hey,

I saw you are looking for a guard dog for protection. Look no further! Meet Killer. Killer is a 4-year-old German-bred attack papillon. I recently acquired him from an ex-Special Forces member who used the dog as his personal protection on dangerous missions across enemy lines. If you are looking for the best of the best when it comes to protection, please consider Killer.

I love Killer, but I have to serve a three-year sentence starting in January and have nobody to care for him. I just want to see Killer put in a good home where he can keep on killin'.

Thanks,

Mike

From Kevin to Me:

that dog sounds bad ass! forgive me but i've never heard of a papillon before. could you send me a picture of him so i can see what he looks like? thank you!

From Me to Kevin:

No problem, Kevin.

I've attached a picture I managed to take of Killer. He hates cameras so it was hard to get a good picture of him (seeing how he is ex-Special Forces, I don't blame him).

Attachment:

From Kevin to Me:

you cant be serious. that thing must be like 10 pounds! no offense but that little dog cant guard shit!!

From Me to Kevin:

Kevin,

No offense taken. He may look small, but he is very deadly. He lures intruders in with his small size and cuteness, and then he brutally mauls them. I live in a bad part of Philly and my home is often subject to break-ins because I am a flat-screen TV collector. The last time a guy tried to break in, Killer bit through his Achilles tendon and caused him to fall onto a fireplace poker that stabbed him through the neck. Trust me: Killer is nothing to mess with. I've even trained him to fire my Glock for the next time an intruder comes.

Mike

From Kevin to Me:

im calling bullshit. anyone could punt that damn tiny dog across the room before he bites through your foot. how in the world can it fire a glock? get real dude

From Me to Kevin:

Kevin,

Trust me, he is an excellent shot. He can keep his shots grouped within 0.2 inches at 50 yards. I usually just have him push the gun around with his nose while he walks, but I find he is more accurate with this device I have come up with. It is a collar that attaches the gun to him and allows him to pull the trigger by biting on a pen that is placed in front of his mouth and across the trigger. It is surprisingly effective. I have trained him on semi-automatic handguns, so if you own one he probably can use it. We are currently working on a .357 Magnum but he is having trouble reloading it. Regardless, Killer will be the most effective guard dog you can ever own.

I've included pictures if you don't believe me.

Mike

Attachments:

From Kevin to Me:

this is fuckin crazy. ive had enough of this, dont email me anymore.

Those pictures were very difficult to take.
My dog was scared shitless and didn't want to be anywhere near that gun. I had to stuff the barrel with bacon to attract him to it.

I'm lucky the guy didn't take me up on my offer,
because then I would have had to train Killer to shoot the gun.

Counterfeit Receipt

I don't know what this guy needed the receipt for, but I assumed it was for something illegal. As a law-abiding citizen, I decided it was my duty to stop him.

Original ad:

> i need a receipt for a 40 inch samsung LCD tv purchased at walmart. the model number is LN40B530 thanks

From Me to ********:

Hey! I recently purchased that TV and still have the receipt for it. I do not plan on returning it because the TV is simply amazing. I have no problem giving you the receipt if you need it.

Thanks,

Mike

From ****** to Me:**

hey great thanks man when can i pick it up?

From Me to ********:

Actually, I can just scan it and send it to you if you want. I have a scanner here in my office and it would be no problem. Is that okay with you?

Mike

From ******** to Me:

yeah sure

From Me to ********:

Okay, I've attached it. Enjoy.

Attachment:

WALLMART
shoping receit

items u bought:

```
1 HDIM cable ............$39.99
1 tv stand ...............$77.35
12 pck trogen condoms ......$11.99
1 samsong 40 inch LDC tv..$921.31
```

GRAND TOTAL!..........$999.99

```
ur cashiers name was:  tyronda
```

THANK U FOR SHOPING AT WALLMART.!

REFUNS POLICEY:

```
if u dont like the stuff u boght
u can give it back to us and get
ur money back its no big deal
```

From ******** to Me:

what the fuck is that you damn fucktard. thats not the real fuckin receipt

From Me to ********:

I don't understand. That is the receipt I got when they rang me up at the register. It looks real to me.

From ****** to Me:**

what part of that looks fuckin real to you? "shoping receit"? "wallmart"? walmart has one L idiot. i dont think you spelled one fuckin thing right. what the fuck are "trogen" condoms? samsong? i guess they dont have spellcheck in ms paint huh?

From ****** to Me:**

oh and by the way your math fuckin sucks!! it looks like you tried to add everything up and gave up and just put $999.99! fuckin moron

From Me to ******:**

I'm sorry that you are so angry. I was just trying to help. Maybe the cashier Tyronda didn't know how to spell anything when she wrote up the receipt. I believe your issue is with Walmart, not with me.

I guess I should work on my Photoshop skills.

Hard to Reach

Original ad:

> im selling my 1991 ford f150 for $2500.
>
> call ***-***-**** for more info or email

From Me to ********:

Hey,

I am interested in your truck. How many miles does it have on it?

Mike

From ******** to Me:

do you have a number you can be reached at?

From Me to ********:

Yes I do. My number is ***-492-159.

From ******** to Me:

that isnt a phone nubmer there arent enough numbers

From Me to ********:

That is my phone number. You can get a number with less digits for a small monthly fee, which I am paying for.

From ******** to Me:

well i dont think its working i tried calling and it said its not a number

From Me to ********:

Did you dial 1 first?

From ******** to Me:

i just tried that and it is not working

From Me to ********:

Wait, are you calling from Philly?

From ******** to Me:

yes

From Me to ********:

Oh, my mistake. Since you are calling from Philly, you have to dial a 6 first, followed by the pound sign, and then my number.

From ******** to Me:

IT ISNT WORKING

From Me to ********:

Shit, do you just want my office number? It is a little complicated.

From ******** to Me:

yeah fine give me that

From Me to ********:

You have to call my office at 215-592-**** and then put in extension 4491-2938 followed by the pound sign to be transferred to the human resources department. Once you are transferred there, you need to enter this security access code: 2A11-3D58-2F41-FW31. You will be put through to Jane our receptionist. She is going to ask you a series of questions to confirm you are not a machine. Upon confirmation, tell her that you want to speak to

Richard. When Richard gets on, tell him Mike sent you and ask him to page me. Use this code as a reference: 8281-WK82F. It should take about two minutes after I receive the page to make it to the secure office phone. I can only talk on that phone for about 15 seconds, so I will give you a randomly generated pay-phone number for you to call me on. I will then run down to the lobby and pick up the pay phone, and then we can talk. Got it?

From ******** to Me:

it says that is not a working number

From Me to ********:

Did you dial 1 first?

From ******** to Me:

fuck this. forget it

From Me to ********:

Wait, I also have a pager number. Do you want that instead?

> This guy really wanted to talk on the phone. He spent more time emailing me trying to get our phone conversation to work than he would have by just emailing me about the truck. The fact that he tried calling the last number I gave him makes me think he was really willing to do all of those security protocols just to talk on the phone. If I had had more time, I could have actually set up some kind of answering machine maze for him to deal with.

Happily Married Couple

For this email exchange, I set up two email accounts: Mike and Jessica Partlow, the happily married couple looking to buy a vacuum cleaner.

Richard's original ad:

> Dyson vacuum in good condition.
>
> Asking $75 or best offer.

From Mike Partlow to Richard:

CC: Jessica Partlow:

Hello,

My wife and I are looking to purchase a vacuum. Is your vacuum still for sale?

Mike

From Richard to Mike Partlow & Jessica Partlow:

Yes, Mike, I am still selling my vacuum. I am asking $75 for it.

From Mike Partlow to Richard & Jessica Partlow:

Great! $75 seems a little expensive for a vacuum, but my wife tells me that Dyson is a great brand. We already have a vacuum, but the house is still dirty. I blame it on my wife's lack of cleaning skills, but she insists it is the vacuum, so we would like to purchase your vacuum in the hopes that my wife will actually clean the house with it.

From Richard to Mike Partlow & Jessica Partlow:

Well, she is correct, Dyson makes quality vacuums and this one is well worth the investment. When would you like to come pick it up?

From Jessica Partlow to Richard & Mike Partlow:

Richard, your vacuum sounds wonderful. Maybe if my alcoholic husband would stop tracking mud and glitter from strip clubs all over the floors, I wouldn't need a new vacuum to clean all the time.

From Mike Partlow to Richard & Jessica Partlow:

Maybe if my premenstrual wife would actually put out every now and then, I wouldn't have to go to strip clubs and jerk off in the shower. Please excuse her comments, Richard. She tends to mouth off a lot and doesn't realize that it may result in her getting another black eye.

From Richard to Mike Partlow & Jessica Partlow:

I don't really care about your marriage problems . . . when can you get the vacuum?

From Jessica Partlow to Richard & Mike Partlow:

Richard, ignore my husband. He doesn't realize that his smartass comments are going to result in another month without him getting laid.

From Mike Partlow to Richard & Jessica Partlow:

Well, my wife doesn't realize that every time I jerk off in the shower, I blow my load in her shampoo bottle.

From Richard to Mike Partlow & Jessica Partlow:

Hahahahaha holy shit!!!

From Jessica Partlow to Richard & Mike Partlow:

My piece of shit husband doesn't realize that if his pathetic two-inch dick could actually get me off, we would have sex much more often.

From Mike Partlow to Richard & Jessica Partlow:

Maybe my dick is only two inches because it is difficult for me to stay hard when my wife has gained 100 pounds and her breasts have turned into disgusting flapjack tits.

From Jessica Partlow to Richard & Mike Partlow:

Go fuck yourself, Mike!

From Richard to Mike Partlow:

Okay, are you guys actually going to buy this vacuum? Can you please stop including your wife in these emails?

From Mike Partlow to Richard & Jessica Partlow:

Yes, Richard. The vacuum can probably suck harder than my wife does when she gives her pathetic blow jobs.

From Jessica Partlow to Richard & Mike Partlow:

Don't worry, dickhead, you'll never get another blow job from me again.

From Richard to Mike Partlow & Jessica Partlow:

Seriously, you two are just wasting my time now. Perhaps your money for the vacuum would be better spent on marriage counseling.

I hope I made it as awkward for Richard as possible. Notice how he told me to stop including my wife in the emails. That means he is siding with me! He was basically telling my wife "Stay out of this, bitch. Men are busy talking."

Happy Meat

I don't know how anyone can tell the difference between meat that came from a happy cow and meat that came from a pissed-off cow. Whether the cow I'm eating was raised in the Playboy mansion or was raised by getting kicked around every day, it still tastes equally delicious to me.

Original ad:

> We want to buy some fresh, organic, humanely raised, happy meat. Cows, pigs, chicken, doesn't matter.

From Me to ********:

Hi,

Are you still interested in fresh meats? I have a wide choice of hard-to-get livestock. Our meats are free from steroids, hormones, and genetically modified foods.

We are unique in that we can provide meats ready to eat similar to the Japanese delicacy of "shirouo," which is a fish served while still alive.

At Anderson farms we took this one step further and perfected the art of cooking and serving meat while the animal is still alive.

We are famous for our live baby veal fully cooked while still alive. We do this by increasing the blood flow to the head while the calf is broiled inside a 200-degree oven. The calf's head is completely outside the oven, and drained blood and cool oxygen are pumped into the calf's brain through tubes. The calf is humanely cooked in comfort, while cool damp towels are wrapped around its head. The calf is cooked to perfection and can be served to your guests on a large tray. Imagine the delight of your guests when they see the live calf smiling at them while being cut up and served. The calf can live for one hour after the tubes are pulled out, giving plenty of time for lively conversation and consumption while it is alive.

This is just one of our selections. Please let me know if you are interested. We take Mastercard and Visa.

Mike

From ******** to Me:

you're an asshole

Neighbor's Car for Sale

I came across this ad with several pictures of the car the guy was selling. I noticed that in one of the pictures, all the way in the distance across the street, there was a beautiful minivan. I had to have it.

Curt's original ad:

> 1995 Civic for sale. 180,000 miles, good condition. CD player and new tires. See pics below.

From Me to Curt:

Hey,

I am replying in regards to your ad for the 1995 Honda Civic for sale. I am not interested in the Civic, but I am interested in the Ford Windstar in the background in the third picture. How much do you want for that? Am I correct in guessing that it is a 1996? You did not post how many miles the van has but it appears to be in good condition.

Thanks,

Mike

From Curt to Me:

That van is not for sale. It is our neighbor's van, which you can see as it is located in the driveway across the street in the picture.

From Me to Curt:

How do you know they are not selling it or willing to sell it? Can you ask them if they will take $2,000 for it?

From Curt to Me:

No, you idiot. They have four kids and I doubt they want to sell it.

From Me to Curt:

I see you are a tough negotiator on their behalf. I will give them $2,100 for it.

From Curt to Me:

Look, retard, did my ad say anything about a van for sale? NO. I'm selling my Civic not my neighbor's fucking van!

From Me to Curt:

Well, maybe you should remove the van from the picture to avoid any confusion in the future. Can I have your neighbor's number so I can talk to them about their van?

From Curt to Me:

Yeah, it's 215-EAT-SHIT.

From Me to Curt:

I tried calling the number but I got a recording saying that it is not a working number. Are you sure you got the number right? Maybe they changed numbers. If that is the case, could you go over to the neighbor's house and get their new number?

From Curt to Me:

Fuck off, you fucking retard.

> If the owners of that Ford Windstar are reading this, please contact me. I am still interested in it, regardless of your very rude neighbor.

Vintage Liquor

From Me to Evan**:**

Hey there! I saw your ad and have some "vintage" liquor you may be interested in.

I have about half a handle of Captain Morgan's Rum, a rare vintage rum from the Caribbean. I bought this at a liquor store on Long Island in 2007, and I believe that its taste has really aged to perfection. I am willing to sell this for $300.

I also have a very rare bottle of Aristocrat Tequila. You can taste the fine vintage in every sip. I acquired it from a friend who says he bought it at a liquor store in Baltimore in 2005. You can really taste that southern atmosphere in this one! Due to its rarity, I will sell this for $500.

Also, if you are interested, I have about half a case of vintage Natural Ice beer. It was acquired from a frat party I was at about a month ago. This frat has a very old history with Syracuse University and that history came with the beer. It doesn't get much more vintage than this. I will part with this at $50 per can.

I really hate to see this stuff go, but after my third DUI, the court ordered me to do a program that involves me staying sober, so I think it is best that I part with this rare liquor.

Please let me know if you are interested. I have several other buyers lined up, so I will need to know very soon.

Thanks, Tim

From Evan to Me:

Tim,

You must be crazy to consider that bottom-end liquor "vintage." I am not interested and am insulted that you would even try to sell me such cheap liquor at such ridiculous prices.

Evan

From Me to Evan:

Evan,

I am very disappointed that you are not interested in these vintage treasures. Every bottle and can I sell comes with priceless historic value. Please reconsider, because I don't think you will find an offer like this anywhere else.

Tim

From Evan to Me:

Are you nuts? You want to sell me beer you stole from a frat, that is a month old, for $50 a can? I am NOT INTERESTED.

From Me to Evan:

I did not steal that beer, and I resent the accusation. Please reconsider purchasing this. I am a recovering alcoholic, and I fear that I will drink again if I am unable to get rid of this booze. Please do not make me drink again!

From Evan to Me:

Why don't you just throw the booze away? You have problems, man.

From Me to Evan:

WJKAJF EVAN U RUNED MY LIF. I DRNK ALL THE BOTTLE. U MADE ME CRSH MY CAR AND RUN AWAY NOW POLICE RJSGJKEW. WIFE IN HOSPTAL. I HATE U EVEN U DISTROY LIFE

I think Evan realized toward the end that I was only trying to be a liquor connoisseur in order to help my problem with alcoholism. He even suggested that I throw my booze away, but then I just took a shit all over his attempts to help me. Sorry, Evan, some people just can't be saved.

Practical Joker

Adam's original ad:

> This waffle iron is in excellent condition.
>
> Teflon aluminum grids. $30.

From Me to Adam:

Hi there! I am looking for a waffle iron for a practical joke, but I was wondering how hot it gets. I don't want my victim to get hurt too badly.

From Adam to Me:

It gets really hot . . . I don't know what your joke is but you probably shouldn't use it.

From Me to Adam:

Well, I guess I'll explain the joke and get your opinion. I have a blind friend, Ryan, and we are always playing practical jokes on each other. Ryan recently pranked me by putting a whoopee cushion under my seat, so I want to get him back.

Ryan likes to play the piano, so I want to heat up the waffle iron and put it where the piano keys are. When he goes to play the piano, I'll wait for him to put his hands on the waffle iron, and then I'll slam it shut on his hands, followed by a smack to his face. He'll be in for a "burning" surprise (heh heh).

So what do you think? Will it be harmless, or does the iron get too hot?

From Adam to Me:

That is an extremely messed-up joke. I would advise against it . . .

all he did was trick you with a whoopee cushion and you are going
to severely burn his hands.

From Me to Adam:

It isn't just the whoopee cushion: a few weeks ago he scared me
by hiding a fake spider in my car. I need to get him back for this
humiliation.

If you don't think the waffle iron prank is a good idea, I have a
couple of other pranks I was thinking of. It should be really easy to
prank him because he is blind. I was thinking of setting a bear trap
on his staircase and putting a bunch of rat traps at the bottom of
the stairs. If the prank goes well, he should step on the bear trap
and then fall into the rat traps, in a hilarious act of revenge. I was
thinking I could still use your waffle iron for this prank . . . perhaps
to lure him downstairs with the smell of waffles.

From Adam to Me:

You are seriously messed-up in the head . . . I wouldn't be able to
sell you this waffle iron and have a clean conscience knowing you
are going to maul a blind man with it.

From Me to Adam:

Well, you just lost a good sale, sir. You obviously can't appreciate a
good practical joke. I guess I'll just go with my classic "gun-powder
in the cigarette" prank, which does not require a waffle iron.

As it turns out, Ryan quit smoking so I was unable to get him with
my cigarette prank. Instead, I tricked him into thinking I was driving
him somewhere, when really I just put the car in neutral and rolled it
down a hill, into the side of a building. When I went to visit Ryan in the
hospital the next day, we both had a good laugh.

Racist Microwave Buyer

I was recently looking online for a microwave, since mine broke (apparently you can't microwave a frozen beer can to thaw it). I came across this ad and was immediately more offended than I have ever been in my entire life.

Amy's original ad:

> ## WANTED—MICROWAVE
>
> I am looking for a used microwave. WHITE ONLY.

From Me to Amy:

I have an LG microwave that I want to sell for $30. I am aware that your ad said whites only, but I am an African-American. I sincerely hope that this won't be a problem for you, and we can put race issues aside and just do business.

Thank you,

Jamal

From Amy to Me:

I am so sorry that you misread my ad. I meant the microwave should be white, because it would match my kitchen.

Amy

From Me to Amy:

Oh, so because I am black, you think that I can't read? It really is amazing that the world we live in is still so racist. I'm sorry, but your insults have left me feeling sick. I don't think I can sell my microwave to a bigot.

Sincerely offended,

Jamal

From Amy to Me:

I wasn't suggesting that you couldn't read. I'm not racist. If you read my whole email, you would see that the ad was looking for a white microwave, not a white person. I changed the ad to avoid any confusion.

Amy

From Me to Amy:

So now you think that because I am black, I am too lazy to read your whole emails. Your racism is overwhelming. You will never get my microwave from me. I will, however, sell you a burning cross for your next klan meeting. Does $20 for the cross sound fair?

From Amy to Me:

I can't write anything without you being offended! I give up!

From Me to Amy:

So you don't want the microwave?

From Amy to Me:

Will you still sell it to me?

From Me to Amy:

I would never sell anything to a racist.

From Amy to Me:

Ugh, I'm done with you.

She may be whistling a different tune now but maybe next time Amy won't be so prejudiced when deciding which race she would like to sell her microwave to. African-Americans need to heat their food too, Amy.

Happy Camper

> trying to go camping and want to purchase a small camper that can be attached to a truck. camper must be clean and in good condition and must be able to sleep at least four people

From Me to Shane:

Hi! I am selling a camper if you are still interested.

Thanks, Mike

From Shane to Me:

yes thank you do you have any pics and what kind of camper is it and how big is it

From Me to Shane:

I am not sure of the brand, as I do not know much about campers, but it is the kind that would attach to the back of a pickup truck. It has a stove, refrigerator, bathroom, mattress, pull-out couch, and dining area. I acquired it at a police auction but have no real use for it.

From Shane to Me:

is it in good condition

From Me to Shane:

I'd say it is. As I said, I got it "as is" from a police auction. I was informed that it used to be a meth lab, which makes sense because there are still jars of chemicals, weird chemistry equipment, and nasty stains everywhere. There is also a very pungent odor. I think the previous owners were in some kind of shoot-out with the authorities, because the door appears to have been bashed in with a battering ram and there are several bullet holes throughout the trailer. I'm not quite sure, but I think there is also a dried pool of blood on the carpet.

I've done my best to patch the bullet holes with stucco, and I have sprayed Fabreeze all over the chemicals to make them safe. As for the door, I put Velcro on it so it will stay shut. I also put a floor mat over the blood stain so you cannot notice it.

From Shane to Me:

not interested why the hell would you buy that in the first place

From Me to Shane:

I bought it as a "handyman's special." That's what I do: I buy things, fix them, and resell them. I may have been mistaken about it being a meth lab; the chemicals might actually just be for some chemistry project. This camper is great if you have kids who are into chemistry.

Would you like to stop by and check it out? I'm asking $1500 for the camper. I'll also throw in a half-full 40 of malt liquor I found in the fridge.

From Shane to Me:

yeah, some handyman you are. a handyman that uses stucco and velcro to fix things wow you should have your own reality show

From Me to Shane:

Well, I always thought about being on TV, but I didn't want to make the other shows look bad by showing off my superior skills. Anyway, when do you want to stop by and look at the camper?

From Shane to Me:

i was being sarcastic you dipshit i dont want that piece of crap camper

Snowblower Accident

A decent snowblower costs about a thousand dollars. I wanted to show this guy what kind of snowblower he could get for a hundred.

Warren's original ad:

SNOWBLOWER WANTED

want cheap snowblower not paying more then $100

From Me to Warren:

Hello,

I have a snowblower that I need to get rid of quickly. I will sell it to you for $100. Will you be able to come get it today?

Thanks,

Mike

From Warren to Me:

yes i can get it today. does it work properly?

From Me to Warren:

I'm not quite sure. It was working this morning. I was going to surprise my neighbor by snowblowing her driveway because she lives alone and is too old to shovel. While I was snowblowing her sidewalk, I think I accidentally ran over her dog, because a bunch of blood and fur started spraying out of the top of the snowblower and onto her front door. I shut the snowblower off and got the hell out of there, and now I need to get rid of the snowblower before she comes over here and questions me. I have been afraid to start it up. It looks like it is in good shape, but it has blood all over it and there are some bones, hair, and guts or something clogging the internal blades. If you can clean that out, it should probably work.

From Warren to Me:

holy shit

From Me to Warren:

I know, right? So can you please come get it very soon?

From Warren to Me:

no sorry man your on your own

From Me to Warren:

Come on, Warren. You aren't going to find a snowblower any cheaper than this. Please come get it.

From Warren to Me:

no you asshole just throw it out its fucked

From Me to Warren:

I can't leave it down at the bottom of my driveway for the garbage truck. My neighbor will see it and know what happened. Please—I have no other way to get rid of it.

> Warren did not help me out at all. I decided that I had to do the right thing. I wrote my neighbor a confession that explained what happened to her dog, and then I forged my other neighbor's signature so she thinks it was him.

Exotic Wood

Dennis's original ad:

> I need air-dried or kiln-dried lumber, prefer 8/4 ash or
> maple. Need about 200 board feet.

From Me to Dennis:

Hello,

I have a lot of maple lumber if you are interested.

Mike

From Dennis to Me:

How much do you want for it? What is the thickness and is it air- or kiln-dried?

Dennis

From Me to Dennis:

Dennis,

The wood varies in thickness. Some of the maple pieces have flooring nails in them. I will throw in some other exotic wood, such as chunks of drywall, plywood, plastic floor tiles, and a wooden tabletop. This lot of wood also comes with a kitchen sink, various pipes, an old refrigerator, electrical wires (no copper), chunks of sheetrock, and an old oven. All of these pieces have been air-dried in my backyard for about two weeks.

I am asking $200 for everything.

Mike

From Dennis to Me:

Only $200 to remove your debris from a kitchen renovation? What a deal.

From Me to Dennis:

Dennis,

I'm glad you have an eye for value. I have had several other people showing interest so I suggest you come down here to buy it quickly.

Thanks,

Mike

From Dennis to Me:

How about you pay someone to get rid of your trash, you fucking moron. The only thing of value in that shit would have been the copper but you already know that. Fuck off.

Dennis missed out on a great bargain. Whatever project he needed the wood for, I am sure it would have looked great with an old oven and refrigerator as well.

Paintball Gear

Let's see how long it takes before this guy completely loses his shit . . .

Gary's original ad:

> I want cheap paintball gear call or text me ***-***-****

From Me to Gary:

Hi,

Still looking for cheap paintball gear? I have cheap gear. I am using a 12-inch rubber band that can be used as a slingshot. It is very accurate. I once took down a robin while it was eating a worm. The robin never saw it coming, and the paintball caused a small explosion of feathers. Heh, I still laugh about it. The price is $49.99 with normal shipping included. How are you fixed for paintballs?

Mike

From Gary to Me:

wtf is ur problem? PAINTBALL not RUBER BANDS

From Me to Gary:

Gary,

Yes, paintballs shot with a very big rubber band. Like I said, when used properly, the rubber band can be deadly. So what is the next step? Do you have PayPal?

Mike

From Gary to Me:

NO i dont have paypal and im not buying this from you, im pro not a kid. Go online and learn something about paintball

From Me to Gary:

There are many benefits to using an extra-strength rubber band to shoot paintballs instead of the common CO2-powered gun. First off, you never run out of gas, which is quite an edge during the heat of battle. Secondly, as General Patton once said, "Stealth is the key to killing." The rubber band I am selling is completely silent; your opponents will never know what hit them. No pressure, but the price I quoted you is my 2009 price, and come January, the price will rise to $59.95. You will need to act quickly. I will accept a money order.

Mike

From Gary to Me:

why dont you do us all a favor and go fuck yourself

BMW Wanted

David's original ad:

WANTED: 2002 or newer BMW low miles will pay up to $15,000

From Me to David:

Hey,

I am trying to sell my 2002 BMW E46 and noticed your ad looking for one. It has been a great car for me, but I recently upgraded and have no use for it anymore. It ran great, has low miles, and looks practically new.

It was involved in a MINOR fender bender, but you should be able to buff it out with no problem. I've attached pictures of the damage, but it really isn't that bad. Let me know what you think.

Thanks,

Tim

Attachments:

From David to Me:

are you fucking kidding me?

This email exchange is short, but I know that at least for a few seconds I got this guy's hopes up, only to disappoint him immediately. The sad part is that people actually do try to sell totaled cars this way.

Eagles Tickets

Original ad:

EAGLES GIANTS MEADOWLANDS SUN DEC. 13 TWO TICKETS! $200 or best offer

---

From Me to *********:

Hey,

I can't believe the Eagles are playing! I haven't seen them in years. Is Joe Walsh still with the band? I will give you $200 cash if I could take my son to his first Eagles concert.

Thanks so much,

Mike

From ****** to Me:**

NOT THE EAGLES BAND ITS THE FOOTBALL TEAM

From Me to *********:

I don't understand . . . why would you try to trick me with your ad?

I already told my son that he was going to his first Eagles concert and he was so excited. You should have seen the smile on his face. Now I am going to have to tell him that you lied to me.

Thanks, asshole.

From ****** to Me:**

THE AD SAYS EAGLES AND GIANTS . . . WHAT THE FUCK ELSE COULD THAT MEAN

THE PHILLY EAGLES VS THE NY GIANTS AT MEADOWLANDS WHICH IS WHERE THE GIANTS PLAY

From Me to *********:

I thought you were trying to say that The Eagles, who are rock and roll "giants," were going to be playing in the Meadowlands. Your ad did not mention football anywhere. It is a damn shame that you tricked me, but to trick my son, that is just plain sick and evil. If you have any shred of decency, you will buy me and my son tickets to The Eagles (the band) concert.

Hoping you'll do the right thing,

Mike

From ******** to Me:

DAMMIT IM NOT TRYING TO TRICK YOU

ANYONE CAN READ THAT AD AND KNOW WHAT I MEANT. YOUR A DUMBASS AND ITS YOUR FAULT THAT YOU TOLD YOUR SON

From Me to *********:

Well, excuse me for thinking that I was dealing with an honest person and not a deceitful wordsmith who tricks people with his ads. Karma will come back to bite you in the ass one day, my friend.

From ******** to Me:

NO IT WONT

EAT SHIT

It would have been awesome if he actually felt bad and bought me tickets to see The Eagles. Would I have taken them? Of course.

Apologetic Nationals Fan

> I am trying to get 2 tickets to the Nationals vs. Red Sox
> on Thursday, June 25th. I'm willing to pay up to $40.

From Me to Austin:

Hello, I do not have tickets to the Nationals, but I do have a videotape of my 7-year-old's Little League team game last week. He plays for the Arby's Allstars, and they beat the Smith Hardware Little Leaguers. I am sure it will be way more entertaining than watching the Nationals get their ass whomped for the 49th time this season.

From Austin to Me:

Fuck yourself, asshole.

From Me to Austin:

Austin, my 7-year-old son was on the computer and he read your very offensive email. Now he is going around telling everyone to "fuck yourself." Me and my wife tried to raise him to be a kid who doesn't curse, but thanks to your profanity, he thinks it is okay. I demand an apology from you.

From Austin to Me:

You want my apology? Go fuck yourself.

From Me to Austin:

I did have the tickets; I was just messing around with you. They were good seats—10 rows back from third base. I was going to sell them both for $30. I would rather burn them, however, if you don't apologize. If you do apologize, the tickets will be yours.

From Me to Austin:

I'm waiting . . .

From Austin to Me:

I'm sorry about your kid.

From Me to Austin:

Hah, what a sucker. I made you look like a little bitch in front of my 7-year-old son. I don't actually have any tickets. Thanks for helping me teach my son a lesson about how not to keep your dignity.

Mike

As if being a Nationals fan wasn't humiliating enough. To be fair, they did beat Boston 9 to 3 in that game. Perhaps Austin was better off watching the actual game instead of my videotape.

Escalade Bodyguard

Edgar's original ad:

> 2007 CADILLAC ESCALADE FOR SALE—38,000 miles.
> Great condition! Asking $40,000. Email if interested.

From Me to Edgar:

Hey,

I have a proposition for you. I will give you $50 if you let me borrow your Escalade for tomorrow night. I have been trying to get a date with this girl, but the only way I was able to get her to go on a date with me was by telling her that I am a very rich and powerful drug dealer. The problem is, I am not a drug dealer, and I actually drive a '91 Honda Accord. She will know I am lying if I pick her up in that. The only chance I have of getting with this chick is if I roll up in your ballin' Escalade. If you let me borrow it, on top of giving you $50, I will put a few gallons of gas in it. I promise we will not have sex on your seats.

Please help me out!

Mike

From Edgar to Me:

Absolutely not. The car is not for rent!

From Me to Edgar:

Edgar,

I am willing to pay you up to $60 to borrow your Escalade. If you are worried about me messing it up, you can ride with me. In fact, you can drive it. I'll tell her you are my bodyguard. That would actually work out better, I think. Do you look like a bodyguard? You'd have to wear a suit and possibly one of those earpieces with the coiled cord running down your neck. You should occasionally touch the earpiece to your ear, like you are listening to some badass security chatter. You shouldn't have to talk much, just drive and look badass.

Please reconsider my offer.

Mike

From Edgar to Me:

No. That is stupid. Maybe you should try asking out a woman that isn't a materialistic gold digger.

From Me to Edgar:

Gold digger or not, this girl's rack is phenomenal. Tell you what— if you consider my offer and I end up getting laid, I will try to snap a picture of her tits with my cell phone and send it to you. Trust me, they are great.

From Edgar to Me:

Shut up. You aren't borrowing my car.

From Me to Edgar:

Well, Edgar, you are being a cockblocker. I hope next time you are trying to get your D wet, you get the shit cockblocked out of you.

> If I have learned anything from my years of dating women, it is that the key to a woman's heart is money and material objects. I thought that my clever idea of renting a life of luxury would lead to years of hot sex with women, but this guy quickly shot down all my hopes and dreams.

Stained Chair

Jeff's original ad:

comfortable office chair in good condition for sale.
black cloth. $15

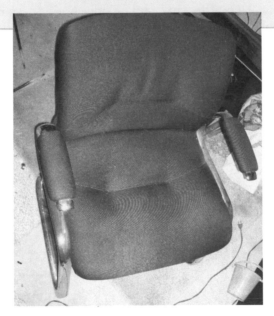

From Me to Jeff:

Hello,

I am interested in your chair for my office. I just am a little concerned about the white stains shown in your picture of the chair. What happened in that chair? Do I even want to know?

Thanks,

Mike

From Jeff to Me:

Those are not stains. The picture of the chair isn't clear enough, but there are no stains on the chair. The chair is in almost new condition. Sorry if the picture isn't clear.

From Me to Jeff:

Jeff,

I don't think you realize what I am talking about. I have circled it in the picture so you can see what I am asking about.

Thanks,

Mike

Attachment:

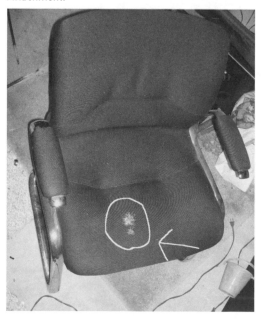

From Jeff to Me:

What . . . that isn't there

From Me to Jeff:

Yes, it is. How can you not see it?

> He didn't respond, so I decided to fuck with him
> with a few more email accounts.

From Me to Jeff:

Hi there! I really need some chairs for my upcoming dinner party and am interested in your chair. Could you tell me what that white stain is on the chair? I don't want my guests to be grossed out. Thanks!

From Jeff to Me:

There is no stain on the chair!

From Me to Jeff:

Yes there is, it is clearly in the picture. Did you get a little lonely in your office or something? I just want to know what the stain is. If it is what I think it is, please just be honest. It is nothing to be ashamed about, just clean up next time.

From Jeff to Me:

What is this! Why is everyone on the internet crazy?!

From Me to Jeff:

If you want to stay in denial, fine. I'll buy my chair somewhere else.

> One more email account, for good measure.

From Me to Jeff:

Hey what is with that stain on your chair?

From Jeff to Me:

THERE ISN'T A FUCKING STAIN!!!

Poor Jeff was probably so confused. I bet he looked over every inch of that chair to see what stain everyone was talking about.

World War II Memorabilia

From Me to Tyler:

Hi,

I have a bunch of World War II stuff that I am trying to get rid of. My grandfather finally passed away and I want to get all his crap out of my attic. Are you still interested? I have several items that are probably very valuable.

I have an authentic baseball circa 1941 that was personally signed by Adolf Hitler. It was used for the first pitch at the annual Third Reich "Bausbaulen Meisterschaft" (Baseball Championship) between the Auschwitz Annihilators and the Berlin Blitzkriegers.

I also have a Russian coin that was used in the coin toss to start off the Russia-Germany football championship match.

From that same football match, I have the Russian playbook that was personally signed by Joseph Stalin. It contains many rare plays that are not seen in football anymore.

As for the Pacific front, I have a set of Japanese bones that were recovered from Nagasaki after the bombing. These bones come with a certificate of authenticity.

Let me know what you are offering for these items.

Thanks,

Mike

From Tyler to Me:

Germany and Russia settled things over a game of American football, eh? Go fuck yourself and never email me again.

I guess he wouldn't have been interested in Winston Churchill's iPod or General Patton's vintage Shelby Mustang either.

Miscellaneous Requests

SOMETIMES I COME ACROSS an ad that is unlike anything I have ever seen before. For example, there was an ad posted by a woman who wanted a complete stranger to expose her children to chicken pox. She was not too pleased when I offered to give them malaria and tuberculosis as well.

This section of the online classifieds also includes the "free stuff" ads. You may be thinking, "Wow! People give stuff away for free? That is wonderful!" That is not the case. You usually won't find anything more valuable than an item you'd find at the dump. For example, an ad for a "free beautiful couch! come and get it!" most likely translates to "come get this goddamn ugly couch out of my living room so I don't have to pay someone to do it." There may as well be an ad saying "Free dog shit! Come and pick up all the dog shit in my backyard and it is yours, for FREE!"

Here you'll also find the occasional personal ad from ugly people looking for sex with a beautiful model, creepy horny people just looking for random sex, and naive people trying to build a trusting and loving relationship with someone they meet on a public website.

There is one untapped section of the personal ads that I cannot touch, and that is the ads for prostitutes. I've got to give the whores credit: they have their shit together when it comes to dealing with assholes like me. They usually refuse emails and will only talk to me if I call them from an unblocked number. However, if someone is looking for sex and would like to discuss it over email, then they have another thing coming.

Black Market Garage Sale

Erica's original ad:

> Having a garage sale starting 10:00 AM on Saturday.
> Many items for sale including electronics and furniture!
> Stop by, at 294 ******** Drive.

From Me to Erica:

Hi,

I saw your ad about a garage sale Saturday and I have some items I would like to sell. I have several TVs, DVD players, and cartons of cigarettes that fell off a truck. I'll set up a table at your garage sale and sell them at discount prices. Your neighbors won't be able to pass up on the deals. What time should I be there to set up my table? How about 8 AM?

Thanks,

Tim

From Erica to Me:

What? You can't sell your stuff at our garage sale. This sale is our family only. You can stop by and check out our stuff if you want, but we aren't letting other people sell things. Sorry.

From Me to Erica:

Erica,

I already told my associates that I found a sale where we can push our items, and I can't back out of it now. Don't worry: if anything, we will attract more customers. Also, my friend Mike has some handguns that he found and needs to sell. I told him he could use some of our space to set up his table. I hope this is okay.

Tim

From Erica to Me:

NO! You CAN NOT SET UP AT OUR GARAGE SALE. If you show up to sell your illegal goods I will call the police. I am serious. Do not come!

From Me to Erica:

Erica,

I am not selling anything illegal. I found all this stuff after it fell off a truck driving through our neighborhood. Tell you what, I'll let you keep a brand-new 42" Samsung 1080p LCD TV. The box was never even opened. Do not call the police. I'll be there at 8 to set up my table.

Tim

From Erica to Me:

THE POLICE WILL BE THERE IF YOU COME. I AM WARNING YOU DO NOT COME TO MY GARAGE SALE

> I don't know what the hell this woman's problem was. If someone offered me a free TV, I wouldn't care where it came from, I would just take it. I wonder how this woman's garage sale turned out. I bet she shit her pants whenever someone showed up who looked remotely like they were from "The Sopranos."

Sexy MILF

This guy had a brilliant idea. Put an ad online, and let all the hot, sexy women come to him. Why didn't I think of that? Here I am trying to pick up women at the bar, like a total dickhead. If I just put an ad up saying I was looking for horny women who want to have sex, I wouldn't have to do any work.

I'll just clarify a few terms (believe it or not, there are still some people who don't know what a MILF is):

MILF: Mother I'd Like to Fuck

DTF: Down to Fuck

NSA: No Strings Attached

Rob's original ad:

> ## HEY BABY GIRL
>
> looking for a good time—NSA. if you are hot sexy and DTF then hit me up

From Me to Rob:

Hey there ;)

I saw your ad and am very interested. You still available?

Alex

From Rob to Me:

yep. got pics? how old are u, where you live?

rob

From Me to Rob:

Rob,

I do not have any pictures, sorry. I am writing to you on behalf of my young beautiful mother (MILF!) who is looking for a man to satisfy her. She lives in North Philly. She is kind of shy, so I am doing this for her. I guarantee she will be worth your while ;)

Alex

From Rob to Me:

uh...how old is she? i need a pic for her. do u have any

rob

From Me to Rob:

She is 94 years old. Her husband (my father) died last year, and she has been lonely ever since. She talks to me all the time about how she hasn't had sex since he passed away. All she wants is a good fuck. She is just having a hard time picking up guys. I took her to the bar a few times, but she ended up getting too drunk and got us thrown out.

Unfortunately the only pic I have of her is from 1937, but she still looks HOT. Do you want that?

From Rob to Me:

are u fuking nuts!!!!!!!

nobody would do that ever!!!!!!!!!!!

From Me to Rob:

Rob, I thought you said you were looking for casual sex. What is the problem here? I know for a fact that she gives it up easily. In the '40s, before she met my dad, she was a total slut. She may be old in age, but she is young at heart and will fuck like a 20-year-old whore.

I don't want her to know I found you through an ad, though. She goes to bingo every Wednesday night—could you go there and start hitting on her? I guarantee once you get a few drinks in her she will be down to fuck.

From Rob to Me**:**

yeah i wanted casual sex not with some dried up old snatch!!! thats fukin gross!!

u need to stop writing to ads and buy her a vibrator problem solved!

From Me to Rob**:**

Man, you sure are picky. Sorry she's not the hot 18-year-old model you were looking for. I saw your picture, and you don't look that good either. I personally think you can't do much better than her anyway. She is probably your only chance to get laid tomorrow. What do you say? Either stay at home with some lotion and tissues, or go to the bingo hall and get some MILF action.

How about you just hook up with her? If you are nervous, it doesn't have to lead to sex right away. Just hook up with her and see where that takes you.

From Rob to Me**:**

stop writing me!!! im sick just thinkng of this!!

Another dickless night for my elderly mother. At least I tried.

Cemented Couch

Original ad:

FREE COUCH!

i have a free plaid couch on the curb outside my house.

the address is 39 ******** rd come and get it!

I can't recall a time that I've looked at a plaid couch and thought, "Wow, that's a really nice-looking couch." I think the only plaid couch I know of is in my redneck friend's backyard, right next to his '78 Squire station wagon that we occasionally throw beer bottles and M-80s at. With my disgust for plaid couches in mind, I think this guy had it coming.

From Me to ********:

Hey. I am tired of driving down ******** and seeing your ugly couch. It is ruining the neighborhood. What the hell were you thinking when you bought that? Nobody is going to want that thing! It better not be there when I drive past tomorrow.

From ******** to Me:

if you dont like it why dont u come and fuckin get it. tough shit if u dont like seeing it. its only been out there 1 day!

From Me to ********:

One day too many. I don't want your shitty couch. Maybe I would if I was a Scottish guy living in the '70s, but I'm not. That couch looks like what would happen if a parrot and a rhino fucked and had a freak baby who grew up and took a shit on your curb. Why don't you pay someone to haul that piece of shit away?

From ****** to Me:**

fuck you buddy! tough shit. drive a different way

From Me to ******:**

I like going that way because it is scenic. Well, at least it was until you put that pile of shit out there. If it is still there tomorrow, I am going to come back during the night and cement it to your driveway.

From ****** to Me:**

COME AND TRY IT MOTHERFUCKER ILL BE WAITING

> I like to think that this guy was up all night, sitting on his porch, intently watching the couch while holding a shotgun.
> What would he tell his wife?
>
> "Honey, what are you doing?"
>
> "I have to watch this couch all night or else some asshole is going to come and cement it to our driveway!"

Free Cabnits!

I tried this idea many times and did not get anyone to fall for it. That is, until I found this dumbass. How could I turn down FREE CABNITS?!

Lashawna's original ad:

FREE CABNITS

CURB ALERT! FREE CABNITS COME GET EM EMAIL FOR PICKUP ADDRESS

There was also a picture of some cabinets, in case you were wondering what the fuck a "cabnit" was.

From Me to Lashawna:

Hi! Am I too late for the cabinets? If not, I can pick them up immediately.

Mike

From Lashawna to Me:

NOPE THEIR URS! IM AT WORK ALL DAY BUT U CAN JUST GO PICK IT UP

MY ADRESS IS 341 N ******** ST

ENJOY

From Me to Lashawna:

Thanks, Lashawna! I'll be there very soon.

From Me to Lashawna:

What the hell are you trying to pull? I just went over to get your cabinets, and as I was opening a drawer to inspect it, a raccoon jumped out at me and bit my hand. I slammed the drawer on it, but it is still in there. Is this some kind of a sick prank? I'm going to have to go to the hospital and get a tetanus shot.

From Lashawna to Me:

WHAT I DIDNT PUT NO RACOON IN THEIR ALL I DID WAS DRAG IT TO THE CURB

From Lashawna to Me:

IS IT STILL IN THEIR

From Me to Lashawna:

Sorry I haven't gotten back to you. I was bleeding so badly that I had to go to the emergency room. I don't have health insurance, so they stuck me with a bill for $900. I don't have that kind of money. I am going to have to ask that you pay the bill, seeing how this is your fault.

Also, you should go home immediately and get rid of the raccoon so this doesn't happen to any other unsuspecting victims.

From Lashawna to Me:

ARE U FUCKIN CRAZY I AINT PAYING FOR UR BILL!!!!! THAT AINT MY FAULT YOU GOT BIT!!! I CANT LEAVE WORK TIL 9 SO LEAVE THE CABNITS ALONE!!

From Me to Lashawna:

If you aren't going to get rid of the raccoon, then I will. I am going to douse the cabinets with gasoline and burn the raccoon out of there. I'll leave the hospital bill in your mailbox. Please take care of it within a week; otherwise it will be reported to collections.

From Lashawna to Me:

NO U STAY THE FUCK AWAY!!!! IM SORRY YOU GOT BIT BUT DONT GO SET A DAMN FIRE ON MY YARD!!!!

From Lashawna to Me:

MIKE U BETTER STAY AWAY I GOT UR EMAIL ADDRESS ILL KNOW WHO TO REPORT IF U BURN IT!!!!!!!

I wonder what Lashawna thought when she came home and saw that her "cabnits" were still there. I'd like to think that she carefully opened every drawer, with some kind of makeshift weapon like a knife tied to a broomstick, ready to stab the raccoon inside.

Also, she spelled "cabinets" wrong three times.
Once was after I spelled it correctly for her.

Free Kittens

> litter of 5 kittens. two orange, two black, one
> mixed-gray. all are three weeks old and looking
> for a good home!

From Me to ********:

hello

i buy all kitten you have. how much?

yin chang

From ****** to Me:**

Sorry. These kittens are not being sold for food.

This was one of the most amazing responses I have ever gotten.
This person immediately figured out what I was trying to imply.

Kittens for My Tiger

To me, there is nobody more fun to mess with than a woman who loves her cats. Somehow, a lot of these cat lovers see right through me.

Shannon's original ad:

> litter of 6 kittens up for adoption! they are all 3 weeks old and are looking for a good home. contact if interested.

From Me to Shannon:

I am interested in taking all six kittens off your hands. How much do you want for them?

Mike

From Shannon to Me:

Mike,

Are you going to take care of all these kittens? I want to make sure they all find a good home, and I was expecting to sell them one at a time. Are you able to house all six of them?

From Me to Shannon:

Shannon,

To be honest, I own a pet Bengal tiger and he is on a strict diet of cats. I usually feed him one cat every couple of days, so this litter should hold him over for a while. Don't worry, though, I'll take good care of the kittens until I feed them to him.

From Shannon to Me:

That is horrible! You will not get a single kitten from me. I really hope you are not serious.

From Me to Shannon:

Shannon,

I was kidding. I seriously need all six kittens, though. Disregard anything I said about a tiger.

From Shannon to Me:

NO.

Shannon probably immediately removed her ad, took all her kittens, and hugged them dearly. Thanks for nothing, Shannon. I had to feed my tiger grown cats instead, which he does not like. He seems to prefer kittens because their innocence makes them even more delicious.

Mexican Roommates

Where I live, it is extremely difficult to sublet an apartment because half the town is trying to do the same thing with their apartments. People looking to sublet will respond to just about anyone who is willing to rent their place, which makes it that much easier for me to get people to respond.

Jared's original ad:

Seeking one more roommate for a 1-bedroom apartment. $475 per month, lease ends mid-August. Utilities included.

From Me to Jared:

Hi. Do you still have room in your apartment for another room—mate? I would like to live there.

Hector

From Jared to Me:

Yes. Rent is $475 per month and includes utilities (electric, water, cable, internet). You would be living with one other person and sharing a bedroom with him. He is majoring in education. There are two beds and plenty of room.

From Me to Jared:

That is very good. Your roommate sounds nice. My major is very close to education, I am majoring in gardening. The rent will be no problem for me. I just have one question—can I bring in a triple bunk bed so that my friends Ricardo and Juan can live there as well? Ricardo and Juan are also gardening majors. We will not get in the way and are very clean.

Hector

From Jared to Me:

Absolutely not. Our lease prohibits more than two people from living in the apartment.

From Me to Jared:

I promise we will not be discovered. If we raise suspicion to any of the landlords, you can tell them that we are just landscapers doing work on your apartment. I told Ricardo and Juan I found a place for them to live, and Ricardo wants to know if his girlfriend can live there as well. Also, would my brother Jose be able to move in? He can just sleep on the couch and Ricardo can share his bunk with his girlfriend.

Hector

From Jared to Me:

NO! Even if you don't get caught, there is not room for that many people.

From Me to Jared:

What is your problem? You aren't even going to be living there next semester so why do you care?

From Jared to Me:

Because I don't want to violate my lease! Go bother someone else before I report you to INS!

From Me to Jared:

No, senor, please don't! Please, I will leave you alone now. No INS.

A few of my friends made the mistake of telling me that they put an ad online to sublet their apartments. I tried this on both of them, but with no success. As soon as I sent the email, I immediately got a call saying "Nice try, Hector." Fortunately, this guy was unaware of my website and believed me.

Spanish Tutor

This ad was right up my alley. I love teaching people, and I am an expert in Spanish from my two years of Spanish in high school.

Julia's original ad:

> Private school in Sacramento seeking experienced Spanish teachers for part-time employment. Classes will be private sessions for adults who wish to learn Spanish. Reply with credentials.

From Me to Julia:

¡Hola! Soy experto de lengua profesional. Tengo gusto de conducir un coche y de comer la fruta. ¿Usted come la cama? El hoy es martes. Prefiero comer el pan. Mi color preferido es azul. ¡Trabajo para usted pronto!

Carlos

From Julia to Me:

Dear "Carlos,"

Thanks for responding to the ad. I don't speak Spanish, but I was able to run what you said through a translator.

"Hello! I am expert of professional language. I have taste to drive a car and to eat the fruit. You eat the bed? The today is Tuesday. I prefer to eat the bread. My favorite color is blue. Work for you soon!"

Good to know what kind of food you eat and what your favorite color is, but I have a strong suspicion that you do not speak the

language at all. Thanks for your application but I am going to have to decline.

Today is Friday, by the way.

From Me to Julia:

¡USTED PUTA! ¡USTED NO TIENE COJONES!

Re: Your Stupid Ad

Occasionally I will see an ad posted in response to another ad. It is usually something along the lines of "Fuck the ad, it is a scam" or "You want something for free? Go fuck yourself." I don't know why the latter isn't just sent directly to the person who posted the original ad. Regardless, I like to respond to these "response" ads pretending to be the original ad that they are complaining about.

In this ad, the guy is criticizing someone else who posted an ad asking for people to write a resume for him.

Kyle's original ad:

RE: WRITE MY RESOMAY

No wonder you can't write your resume yourself; you are a fucking idiot. If you can't even spell "resume" correctly, how can you expect to get a job? Not even a well-written resume could land your dumbass a job. Give it up and become a janitor!

From Me to Kyle:

hey sorry if i dont have time too reed the dictonarie. ooh wow u now how to spel big words like resume resomay who gives a fuk? big fucken deel u ass whole. u fukin doosh bag i shure wont be hireing u to rite my resomay go fuk youre self

From Kyle to Me:

Nobody is going to write your goddamn resume for you, you fucking dipshit. Do you even know what a resume is, or do you just think it is some magical document that gets you a job? How about you get a fucking education before you attempt to enter the job market? God, you're a fucking retard!

From Me to Kyle:

now listen hardley you goddam prik: i now what a resume is and i alredy got my G.E.D. so whose the uneducator now? u now what? i dont need some ecotistical pretendous speling conesore to rite it so fuk off.

B.S. its "goddam" not "goddamn" u doosh bag. it seams u urself need a leson in speling!

From Kyle to Me:

I didn't think that you could cram any more stupid into a single email yet you managed to blow my mind again. Wow, you got your GED. So did millions of other kids when they graduated high school.

P.S. It is "goddamn" and it is "P.S." not "B.S."

From Kyle to Me:

Good news! I wrote you a resume. Be sure to hand this in to get your job!

MIKE PARTLOW'S RESUME

- Dropped on head as a child
- Obtained GED by sucking the dick of a test grader

Past Job Experience

- 1999 to Present: Self-employed, sucked dicks in alleyways for money and blow.

What a nice guy! He didn't have to write all that for me.

Free Standing Punching Bag

Sometimes I'll luck out and find something awesome for free.

Nick's original ad:

> ## FREE STANDING HEAVY BAG—$75
>
> Free standing heavy bag. Comes with boxing gloves.

From Me to Nick:

Hi there,

My son wants to learn how to box and I think this would be perfect for him. When can I come pick it up?

Mike

From Nick to Me:

I'm around for most of the holiday. I am only accepting cash for the bag. Give me a call @ 313-***-****.

Nick

From Me to Nick:

I don't understand. Your ad said it was free, and now you want money for it? What kind of a scam are you trying to pull here? Thanks for nothing. I have to go tell my son that he won't be getting the punching bag.

From Nick to Me:

I did not say it was free. If you read the ad, it says right at the top $75.

From Me to Nick:

That is not what it says. It says "FREE STANDING HEAVY BAG—$75." Which means you are giving away a free heavy bag valued at $75.

This is my first time buying something on the internet and unfortunately it will be my last. I always hear on the news that there are nothing but scammers on the internet and I guess I am just another victim of this disgusting con. I hope you feel good about yourself; my son has not said a word since I told him that he will not be getting the punching bag.

Mike

From Nick to Me:

I am not a scammer. The bag is "free standing," not "free." Free standing means that the punching bag can stand up without chains when you fill the base with sand or water. If you know how the ads work, you'd see that there is a separate section for free items that this punching bag is not in. Don't try to guilt me about your son. It is entirely your fault for misinterpreting the ad.

From Me to Nick:

Nick, when you put "FREE" in the ad, usually it means that the item you are offering is free. Although my knowledge of online classified ads is limited, my knowledge of the English language is much better and I know what the word "free" means.

Are you even really located in Mandeville, or are you really in Nigeria? I will not be a victim of your little scam.

I just checked on my son. He is in the other room watching the "Rocky" training montage and crying. He wanted to be just like Rocky, but now you have crushed his dreams by denying him a punching bag. I am trying to explain to him that not all people are sadistic scammers, but he won't believe me.

Mike

From Nick to Me:

You're a fucking dumbass. I can't explain this to you any better than I already have. You should explain to your son that you are too stupid to understand how to buy things on the internet.

From Me to Nick:

My son wants to write to you. Forgive his spelling errors; he is only ten years old.

hi mr. punchingbag man. why did you lie to my dad? he said i cant have youre punching bag cause you are a bad man. why are you evil?

> I think Nick contemplated cursing me out again, but decided against it in case I was genuinely serious and actually had my kid write to him.

New Relationship

Abusive relationships can be rough. They can make you never trust another person again. But what better way to start a new relationship than to find a complete stranger on the internet?

I apologize for the boring start of the email, but I thought it was necessary to gain this woman's trust.

Christina's original ad:

> Is the right guy out there for me? Finally ended a long and abusive relationship and want to get my life back on track. Looking for a great guy who can treat me like a woman. Email with pictures and a description of yourself.

From Me to Christina:

Hey,

I saw your ad and really think I can relate to you. I just got out of an abusive relationship as well, and although I think it is too soon to be dating again, I am so lonely that I am looking for someone to start over with. I saw that you were also in an abusive relationship, and maybe we can connect through our hard times shared with our exes, but take it slow. A little about myself: I am 27 years old, I live in Denver as well, and am very loving and outgoing. I love to just stay in and watch a movie, rather than going to the club and dancing. I love music and also play the guitar. Maybe we can jam? I'll look forward to hearing from you.

Mike

From Christina to Me:

Hi Mike! I'm Christina. Sorry to hear about your relationship. A bad relationship can really take over your life if you let it.

Let's talk a little more. Do you have any pictures? Do you use instant messaging? We can talk on there, my screenname is ********.

From Me to Christina:

Christina,

Sorry, but I am at work right now and they don't let us use instant messaging. I can email you and still manage to look productive to anyone who walks behind my desk, but instant messaging would be too obvious. I can have pictures for you when I get home in a few hours.

So tell me about yourself! What are your hobbies?

Mike

From Christina to Me:

Well, some people might call me an animal nut lol! I love to go horseback riding, I own two amazing dogs, and I take care of other people's pets for some income. I am a huuuuuuge Pearl Jam fan. I've seen them in concert nine times! I love seeing live music. The Red Rocks Amphitheatre is my favorite place ever! Have you ever been there? What kind of music do you like?

From Me to Christina:

Christina,

That's cool! I haven't been to Red Rocks since I got kicked out for pissing on a guy in a wheelchair during a Phish show.

I couldn't help but notice you didn't mention anything about cooking. Do you like to cook? My last girlfriend never cooked for me and it really irritated me.

Mike

From Christina to Me:

Wow lol how drunk were you?

I enjoy cooking though I wouldn't consider it a hobby of mine. My mother gave me all of the family recipes (we are a traditional Italian family).

From Me to Christina:

Great! I just wanted to make sure you knew your place as far as cooking is concerned. What about cleaning and ironing?

From Christina to Me:

lol are you looking for a girlfriend or a maid?

From Me to Christina:

I'm just looking for a girlfriend who knows that I wear the pants in the relationship, that's all. I just want a nice cooked meal when I get home from work, that I can eat on a freshly cleaned tabletop while you are in the other room ironing my shirts. As long as you understand that I wear the pants, the belt that holds those pants won't have to come off.

From Christina to Me:

I don't like where you are going with this, Mike. I got out of an abusive relationship. I don't want another one.

From Me to Christina:

Relax; this won't be an abusive relationship! I am very kind, sensitive, and loving. I only had to abuse my last girlfriend because she didn't understand that she had to perform her womanly duties. You said you come from an Italian family, so you should know that it is an Italian tradition of keeping the spouse in line if she needs it. I believe this tradition is called "giustizia" in Italy.

I'm home from work now, so I have attached a picture.

Attachment:

From Christina to Me:

. . . uh . . . nice kitchen . . .

From Me to Christina:

It concerns me that you think the kitchen is "nice." It is obviously in need of cleaning. It hasn't been cleaned since my ex moved into that battered women's shelter. I tried to get her to clean it, but apparently that violated my restraining order and I had to spend the night in jail. I'm not saying you have to clean it right after our first date, but if you could do it before you leave the next morning, that would be great. Otherwise, we might have problems . . . you wouldn't want to be in another abusive relationship, would you?

From Christina to Me:

No, which is why I am staying the fuck away from you. You're an asshole. You deserve to be in jail, not a relationship.

420 Friendly

There are a lot of people looking for drugs online, although they can't just come out and say that they want drugs. This girl either wanted weed or was just saying "You have to be cool with me smoking weed around you."

Stacey's original ad:

**26 YEAR OLD FEMALE WHO LOVES MUSIC
LOOKING FOR FRIENDLY MALE CONCERT BUDDY.**

i have tickets to see STS9 tomorrow night and am looking for someone to go with me to see them. you must be 420 friendly!

From Me to Stacey:

Dear potential concert buddy,

I saw your ad and am very interested. I love music. About myself, I am a 25-year-old music-loving male. I see all kinds of concerts and would love to check out STS9. I'm not quite sure what kind of music that is.

I am not sure what you mean by 420 friendly, however. Do you live near route 420? That isn't a problem for me, since it is kind of on the way to Philly anyway. Email me back if you want to go to the show with me.

Thank you,

Tim

From Stacey to Me:

hi tim. i wasn't talking about route 420 . . . you have to be "cool" if you know what I mean.

stacey

From Me to Stacey:

Stacey,

Glad to hear back from you! Unfortunately I am a little confused. I am cool—at least my mother and co-workers say so. So if you want someone who is cool, I am your guy!

Tim

From Stacey to Me:

no i dont think you get me. you need to be down with the chronic lol. ya get me?

From Me to Stacey:

Are you talking about Dr. Dre's album "The Chronic"? I love hip-hop! Is that what kind of music STS9 is? I assure you that I am "down" with that album. You can play it in the car on the way to the show if you like.

From Stacey to Me:

um no . . . okay, i dont think you are the type person i want to go to the concert with, no offense

From Me to Stacey:

Stacey,

I'm not sure why you suddenly decided not to go to the concert with me. I am kind of disappointed, because I just bought an ounce of headies and was looking for someone else to smoke it with. My other friend has tickets to go see Bisco in Baltimore so I guess I'll just go with him.

Sorry we couldn't be friends,

Tim

From Stacey to Me:

wtf are you fucking serious? why were you being so dense about the 420 thing! and wtf you are seeing Bisco but you never heard of STS9?

From Me to Stacey:

I'm not sure what you mean about the "420 thing." What are you talking about?

From Stacey to Me:

ugh nvm

> If Stacey had been more specific, she could have been smoked up with some really good weed.

Barely Legal Little League

> We are a Little League team looking for a sponsor for the upcoming season. Email if you are interested in helping out. Thanks!

From Me to Joe:

Good afternoon,

I came across your ad looking for a sponsor for your Little League team. I am interested if you still need one. Let me know, and we can discuss the details.

Mike

From Joe to Me:

Hey Mike,

My name is Joe. I have been the coach of this team and greatly appreciate the offer. We still do need a sponsor and I would like to hear what you have to offer. The league will not start up again until mid-April so we will have some time. Let me know what you were thinking for sponsorship; you can email or call me anytime at ***-***-****.

Thanks,

Joe

From Me to Joe:

Joe,

I am glad to hear you are still interested. I would like to have my company name on your team's uniform and fence sign. How much would it cost to do this?

Mike

From Joe to Me**:**

Hi Mike,

The cost to fully sponsor our team would be $800. It would cover ordering the jerseys and equipment. At the end of the season you will be recognized at our ceremony and will receive a framed photo of the team and your own uniform. What is your company's name and do you have a website?

Thanks,

Joe

From Me to Joe**:**

That sounds reasonable, Joe. I am the founder of an adult film company called Barely Legal Super Sluts. We specialize in 18+ amateur pornography and I would like to get our name out there. We plan on launching our site around April, so I think the timing would be perfect with your league. I can forward you our logo and we will discuss designs for the uniforms.

Mike

From Joe to Me**:**

Mike,

Do you realize this sponsorship is for a Little League team?

Joe

From Me to Joe**:**

Yes, you told me that. I think it is great that I'll be able to help kids enjoy America's greatest pastime.

From Joe to Me:

And you honestly expect a bunch of kids to be sporting a jersey that says Barely Legal Super Sluts?

From Me to Joe:

Is it too long to fit on the jersey? We could just use Super Sluts for short as long as the sign on the field included the link to our website.

From Joe to Me:

No, that isn't the problem. This team is for kids and we can't have them wearing shirts that say Super Sluts on them. It is highly offensive and the league most likely wouldn't even allow it.

From Me to Joe:

How about we call them the Barely Legal Little Leaguers? I would include a free copy of our "Super Sluts Slurping Loads" DVD for every parent that attends the game. The DVD features over three hours of sluts with hilarious outtakes and alternate endings. I could even have a few of our stars come out and mud wrestle during the seventh inning stretch. I think it could pull in a lot more of an audience for your Little League.

From Joe to Me:

No! That's even worse! Look, Mike, I appreciate you trying to help our team out but this is absolutely the wrong place to be advertising your porn. If you would still like to contribute, you can, but we cannot have your company name associated with our team.

From Me to Joe:

If this is how you treat every sponsor that wants to help your team out, you will never get any money. Sooner or later you are going to have to whore yourself out to someone, which is a valuable lesson learned in my "Big Sluts: Big Loads" DVD. I could give that one out to the parents instead, due to the educational value.

From Joe to Me**:**

You just don't quit, do you? Ain't happening so go to hell!

I'm still hoping this guy can't find anyone to sponsor his team and will have to come crawling back to me. Even though it isn't a real company, I would gladly pay $800 to know that somewhere there is a Little League team that has "Barely Legal Super Sluts" on their jersey.